CLARE McGLYNN AND
KELLY JOHNSON

CYBERFLASHING

Recognising Harms, Reforming Laws

BRISTOL
UNIVERSITY
PRESS

First published in Great Britain in 2021 by

Bristol University Press
University of Bristol
1-9 Old Park Hill
Bristol
BS2 8BB
UK
t: +44 (0)117 954 5940
e: bup-info@bristol.ac.uk

Details of international sales and distribution partners are available at
bristoluniversitypress.co.uk

British Library Cataloguing in Publication Data
A catalogue record for this book is available from the British Library

ISBN 978-1-5292-1762-9 paperback
ISBN 978-1-5292-1763-6 ePub
ISBN 978-1-5292-1764-3 ePdf

Cover design: blu inc, Bristol
Cover image credit: iStock-488435034

Printed and bound by CPI Group (UK) Ltd, Croydon, CR0 4YY

Contents

Acknowledgements

We extend our greatest thanks to the many women who have spoken out about their experiences of cyberflashing. You have brought to everyone's attention the nature and extent of this problem, making politicians, lawyers, the criminal justice system and the public in general sit up, take notice, and demand action. We all owe you a debt of gratitude for your courage and fortitude in coming forward and sharing your stories.

Many of these experiences have only come to light due to the commitment and sensitivity of journalists and campaigners seeking to raise awareness about cyberflashing and generate change. Sophie Gallagher, in particular, has played a central role in giving voice to so many women, as well as bringing this issue to the attention of policy-makers and politicians. Sophie's reporting in the *Huffington Post* has provided a foundation for much of the discussion and analysis in this book. Thanks are also due to the many other journalists who are bringing this issue to the attention of a huge variety of readers and viewers, on many different platforms.

Our approach has also been shaped by working with organisations supporting women who have experienced cyberflashing, and other forms of image-based sexual abuse and sexual violence. Sophie Mortimer of the Revenge Porn Helpline and the End Violence Against Women coalition have helped to shape our approach to what steps are needed to tackle these abuses. The research and advocacy of the organisations Glitch, Imkaan and the Angelou Centre have also influenced our thinking on how we understand this phenomenon, how it may be experienced differently by individuals with varied experiences and identities, particularly black and minoritised women, and how we navigate the balancing of different policy approaches including criminalisation. The Law Commission's work in this area has sparked many insights and ideas and we look forward to continuing debates over the coming years, as we all work towards shared goals of effective, long-lasting and valuable law reform.

We owe an enormous debt of gratitude to two particular colleagues – Erika Rackley and Fiona Vera-Gray – who have discussed the ideas in this book on many occasions with us, who have read many drafts of the text and who have sustained us through this writing process. In particular, the insights and ideas put forward in this book build on our collaborative work. Cyberflashing is a form of image-based sexual abuse and our analysis emerges from the foundational work with Erika on this matter over the last few years. Similarly, Fiona's work on sexual intrusions and our co-authored work on pornography underpins much of our thinking. Thank you both for all your insights, collegiality and support.

The book could not have been written and finalised without Magdalena Furgalska. She has been a stalwart in her dedication as a research assistant. Thank you Magda for your consistent, reliable and insightful help with this and other projects.

Many other colleagues have answered our queries and provided sources, references and ideas, often in response to urgent requests. Thanks to Maria Bjarnadottir, Sandy Brindley, Graeme Brown, Sharon Cowan, Sophie Doherty, Nicola Henry, Susan Leahy, Sophie Mortimer, Ian Ward and Linnea Wegerstad.

Finally, we thank our families for sustaining us through this project and providing the inspiration to work towards a more egalitarian world.

Introduction

Women have had enough. They have been trained to minimise men's harassment and intrusions into their daily lives. They have become accustomed to brushing off experiences that leave them feeling disturbed, uncomfortable and fearful for their or others' safety. They have become habituated to being alert to the conduct of others, just in case: the stranger acting oddly on the train, the group of lads looking over, the man hanging around the shopping centre.

This is such an everyday aspect of life for so many that it has become taken for granted, almost unnoticed that women do this 'safety work' – managing their behaviour, routines, interactions, visibility and conduct in online and offline spaces – all to minimise the threat of men's intrusions and abusive practices (Vera-Gray, 2016; Vera-Gray and Kelly, 2020). But now, more and more women are challenging men's harassment and intrusions, and are seeking education, prevention and redress.

These challenges are now turning to the common practice of cyberflashing – where a man sends an unsolicited penis image to another, commonly a woman. Women experience it on the train, in the supermarket, queueing for coffee and in their everyday interactions online. For many this intrusion is an annoyance, an irritation, but perhaps something they should simply 'shrug off'. But the significance and impacts of cyberflashing must not be minimised. It can also be experienced as violating, deeply disturbing and threatening: Why would someone send this? Who are they? What might happen next?

Recognising women's experiences

Many women with these experiences of cyberflashing have spoken out and are demanding change. In developing our analysis of the nature, extent and harms of cyberflashing, we draw on these publicly available testimonies. These testimonies have been shared in many different media outlets, and we use examples and case studies from the UK, Ireland, the US, Canada, Australia and Singapore, exemplifying the international nature of this problem. This does not mean these are countries where online abuse and cyberflashing is more prevalent, but our study is limited to accessible English language material. This pool of public testimonies is sizeable; for example, 70 women shared their experiences with journalist Sophie Gallagher (Gallagher, 2019a). When engaging with these testimonies, we use the women's names as they appear in the media. In some cases, this is a pseudonym, and in others women use their real names. We follow their choices. Additionally, we use the term 'victim-survivor' to refer to those who have been sent unsolicited penis images, to emphasise the wrong and harm of cyberflashing, while simultaneously recognising the agency, strength and resistance of those who have experienced this abuse (Kelly et al, 1996).

We are, however, limited in what we can say about inter-sectional experiences and harms of cyberflashing, because the public testimonies rarely share personal characteristics, beyond perhaps mentioning gender and age. Therefore, we can say little about the interlocking significance of sexuality, class, race, ethnicity, disability or religion in the context of cyberflashing. It is crucial, therefore, that further research is undertaken to develop an intersectional understanding of cyberflashing (Lumsden and Harmer, 2019; Harris and Vitis 2020). This is particularly because we know that younger women, trans and gender-non-binary women, and/or black and minoritised women are disproportionately subject to online abuse (Glitch UK and EVAW, 2020).

We address women's experiences in this book as they are disproportionately the targets of cyberflashing, with men being the main perpetrators. Accordingly, we use the pronouns 'she/her' to refer to victim-survivors and 'he/him/his' as perpetrators to reflect the gendered dynamics that we address, but without making claims that this is always the pattern. Further, we do not address the distinctive features and experiences of sending and receiving unsolicited penis images in communities of men who have sex with men, gay and bisexual men, and/or trans, queer or gender-diverse individuals (LGBTQI+). While further research is needed, current work indicates the context and experiences of many in these groups is distinct and therefore requires specific consideration and analysis (Tziallas, 2015; Walling and Pym, 2017; Marcotte et al, 2020).

Cyberflashing terminology

We use the term 'cyberflashing', which we define as the digital distribution of penis images or videos to another without the recipient's consent, including flaccid and erect penises, as well as altered and live-streaming images. Our focus is on nude images. We do not include cartoon images because, as we suggest in Chapter two, the harms of cyberflashing are connected with the verisimilitude of the penis image – it's 'real-world' violation of women's sexual autonomy, and the sense of threat it can engender. For the same reasons, we limit our definition to penis images, as the distribution of other forms of sexually explicit material and pornography raise more general concerns and induce different harms. Finally, and to be clear, we exclude consensually shared genital images; our concern is with non-consensual sexual behaviour.

The term cyberflashing first came to the fore in 2015 when it was reported that a woman had been sent penis images via Bluetooth on public transport, with the police confirming it to be the first reported incident of its kind (Bell, 2015; Dean, 2015). Although this is often cited as one of the first cases of cyberflashing, we know that long before this case and 'cyberflashing' was coined, men were engaging in this practice. The Urban Dictionary, for example, provided its first definition of 'unsolicited dick pic' in 2007, not long after the phrase 'dick pic' first appeared (Urban Dictionary, 2020). This suggests cyberflashing has been taking place for as long as men have been harnessing digital technologies to send images of their penis to others.

Although the phrase 'unsolicited dick pics' is often used to describe cyberflashing, we do not use this term because it risks minimising and trivialising these behaviours; 'dick pic' has connotations of 'levity' which belittles cyberflashing and makes it sound like a humorous and harmless practice (Thompson, 2019). This in turn normalises this behaviour and increases its acceptability. Also, while the word 'unsolicited' affirms the uninvited nature of the penis image, the term 'unsolicited dick pic' tends to focus on the image rather than the cyberflashing action and actor, making it less visible who is doing what to whom, and the violation involved in the act.

Accordingly, we instead use 'cyberflashing', a term which identifies the interconnection between the technological nature of the practices (hence 'cyber') and other forms of sexual exposure (also known as 'flashing') (Thompson, 2016; Hayes and Dragiewicz, 2018). This terminology has its own limitations which mostly parallel critiques of the term 'flashing'; 'flashing' minimises the nature and harms of sexual exposure, and is also inconsistent with victim–survivors' experiences. It evokes the idea of a short-lived experience – a flash – yet many recount prolonged in-person encounters, such as when confined and isolated on public transport with the perpetrator (Vera-Gray, 2016, 101–104). The nature of the exposure in cyberflashing is even further removed from that of a 'fleeting encounter' because it involves the perpetrator exposing his penis via a digital photograph or video. In enacting the exposure through such images, the act becomes suspended in time – embodied in a fixed, tangible object that is inserted into victim-survivors' personal devices and digital social worlds. This parallels Powell and Henry's (2017, 135) discussion of the power of images, constituting a visual 'remnant' which exists beyond visual memory. Nevertheless, despite the limitations of the term 'cyberflashing', we continue to use it for want of an equally clear and easily-recognisable alternative phrase.

In labelling these practices as 'cyberflashing', we are conscious that by categorising this as a specific practice, we are separating it from other intrusive behaviours and forms of sexual violence. This risks excluding related practices and lived experiences that are not within our definition. Our aim, though, is to improve recognition and understanding of cyberflashing, making visible its particular significance, as well as the wrong and potential harms it entails (Branigin, 2016; Boyle 2018).

Recognising cyberflashing: Nature, extent and harms

The book is divided into two parts. The first part develops a holistic understanding of cyberflashing, addressing its extent, nature and potential harms, and giving voice to victim-survivors' experiences. We begin in Chapter one by examining the range of circumstances and contexts in which cyberflashing takes place, and what we currently know about its prevalence, and perpetrator motives. Our analysis highlights the gendered and sexualised nature of this abuse, and accordingly, we conceptualise cyberflashing as a sexual intrusion which sits on a continuum with other forms of sexual violence experienced by women and girls.

Chapter two explores the potential harms of cyberflashing. We underline that, fundamentally, cyberflashing infringes sexual autonomy. We then identify the sexual nature of the harm experienced by some victim-survivors, with many characterising their experiences as one of sexual violation or humiliation. We emphasise the 'real-world', cumulative and broader social impacts of cyberflashing, including engendering a significant sense of fear and threat, curtailing women's freedoms and civic participation, and furthering gender inequality.

Reforming the criminal law

Chapter three begins the second part of the book, by engaging with the possibilities and limitations of the criminal law for addressing cyberflashing – recognising the expressive and transformative power of law, but simultaneously its capacity to reinforce disadvantage and oppression, and distract focus from cultural change initiatives. We conclude that, despite concerns with criminalisation, reforming the criminal law must still be part of a project for change, to better recognise the harms of cyberflashing and offer victim-survivors options for redress.

A detailed analysis of English law is offered in Chapter four, demonstrating that the current law is piecemeal, inadequate, failing victim-survivors of cyberflashing, and therefore requires reform.[1] To inform such debates, Chapter five provides an in-depth examination of the criminal laws covering cyberflashing which have been adopted in other jurisdictions, including the US, Singapore, Ireland and Scotland.

Drawing on the analysis and arguments offered in the book thus far, Chapter six justifies the adoption of a bespoke offence criminalising cyberflashing. We set out the parameters of such an offence, emphasising the need to focus on the core wrong of non-consent, and ensure that any new law is effective and enforceable. In addition, we identify further possible reforms, including a more general offence targeting a broader range of intrusive behaviours, as well as the need for a comprehensive review of sexual offence laws.

---

[1]   Where reference is made to 'English law' this includes the law in Wales. Northern Ireland and Scotland are entirely different legal systems, with differing criminal laws, policies and procedures.

Beyond the criminal law

However, reforming the criminal law is only ever the first stage in a project of change. If the criminal law is to be effective in providing justice options for women, victim-survivors must be aware of the law, and have confidence that the police will take their reports seriously. The high attrition rate for sexual offences generally, and image-based sexual abuse in particular, suggests considerable efforts will be needed to ensure police and prosecutors have appropriate training, resourcing and confidence to take reports forward (Bond and Tyrell, 2018; Barr, 2019; Robinson and Dowling, 2019).

Moreover, the expressive power of the criminal law will only be realised if there is a broad package of coordinated and transformative awareness-raising initiatives, such as the 'Report it to Stop it' campaign encouraging the reporting of street harassment (Transport for London, nd; Gekoski et al, 2015). Such efforts must be guided by an empowering sexual ethics approach that prioritises affirmative consent, reciprocity and sexual freedom, and clearly separates penis images sent in consensual contexts from cyberflashing (for example the Empowerment Project's 'Don't be a Dick' campaign, nd). These messages need to be embedded in our schools, universities, and mainstream public discourse, drawing, for example, on resources focusing on digital sexual harassment (School of Sexuality Education, 2020).

It is also imperative that social media and tech companies do more to remove harmful material and develop preventative technology. While some firms are exercising leadership in the fight against unsolicited penis images – such as dating apps Badoo (Strick, 2020) and Bumble (Holmes, 2019) – there is much more that could, and should, be done (Eterovic-Soric et al, 2017; Are, 2020; Henry et al, 2020).

Finally, while our focus is on the significance of cyberflashing and its potentially serious harms, this is not to deny women's capacity to resist, challenge, and survive violence. Increasingly we are seeing women and girls harnessing the online world by engaging in digital justice-seeking practices, such as naming and shaming perpetrators, hashtag activism, and creative and comedic resistance (Fileborn, 2017; Vitis and Gilmour, 2017; Ringrose and Lawrence, 2018; Amundsen, 2020). As Harris and Vitis write (2020, 335), technologies can create 'spaces of violence but also spaces to resist violence'. Indeed, this book has only been possible because victim-survivors have spoken out. These actions of strength and resistance form the foundation of the fight for change, and remain integral to shifting understanding and attitudes towards cyberflashing, helping to reshape law, policy and practice to better reflect and address the everyday experiences of women and girls.

PART I

Recognising Cyberflashing

ONE

Cyberflashing as a Sexual Intrusion: Nature, Extent and Motivations

> People are still treating this as if it's something to laugh off, a bit of fun, but it's not.
>
> (Dawn, quoted in Gallagher, 2020)

Cyberflashing is non-consensual sexual conduct which intrudes on women's privacy, autonomy and everyday lives. It can induce fear, alarm and significant other harms. It can also interfere with daily life on a more mundane but troublesome level, with women having to navigate and anticipate men's conduct and reactions. It therefore inhibits and restricts women's freedoms, as they take steps to avoid being cyberflashed, often at considerable cost to their personal and professional lives. In this light, we suggest that cyberflashing is best understood as a form of sexual intrusion which sits on a continuum with other forms of sexual violence experienced by women and girls.

To develop this argument, this chapter provides a deeper understanding of the nature and extent of cyberflashing, as well as examining the range of circumstances and contexts in which it takes place. We consider first the commonality of cyberflashing, outlining the available prevalence data identifying women, and particularly younger women, as the main targets. We then examine the variety of contexts in which cyberflashing is perpetrated, drawing primarily on the wide range of publicly available testimonies of women who have shared their experiences of cyberflashing, as discussed in the introduction. We consider how women are cyberflashed in public spaces and particularly on public transport, to being bombarded with penis images on dating apps, to intrusions in everyday social media and online interactions. As explained in the introduction, our focus is predominantly on men's perpetration of cyberflashing against women, recognising that sending unsolicited penis images in other circumstances, such as to other men, can involve different contexts and reactions (Tziallas, 2015). We then explore current understandings of the motivations of perpetrators, followed by an outline of our conceptualisation of cyberflashing as a sexual intrusion.

How common is cyberflashing?

There is a shortage of data identifying the extent of cyberflashing, although much needed research in this area is beginning to emerge (Amundsen, 2020; Mandau, 2020; Marcotte et al, 2020; Oswald et al, 2020). These studies have focussed on specific contexts of cyberflashing, such as in dating environments, and involved particular age groups, sexualities or geographic location. They deepen our understanding of specific aspects of cyberflashing, though questions remain regarding overall prevalence. Further, while there are several studies of online sexual harassment, they tend to cover more general themes, making it difficult to identify cyberflashing among other problematic behaviours (Powell and Henry, 2017).

While it is important therefore not to generalise across all populations, these studies consistently find that cyberflashing is a common experience, with women, and young women in particular, disproportionately facing the highest rates of victimisation and disclosing the most negative impacts. One recent UK survey of 2,121 millennial women, for example, found that 41 per cent had been sent a penis picture without consent; for younger women, victimisation was even more common, affecting almost half of women (47 per cent) aged 18–24 years old (YouGov, 2018). This is similar to Marcotte et al's (2020) study of 2,045 US women which found that among women who had received penis images with or without consent (50 per cent), almost all (91 per cent) had received an unsolicited image of a penis. These findings are paralleled in another US study with a nationally representative survey of 4,248 respondents, where 31 per cent of participants had been sent unsolicited explicit images (Pew Research Centre, 2017). Victimisation was unequally distributed, with young women aged 18–29 facing the highest incidence at 53 per cent (Pew Research Centre, 2017). Among even younger groups, a considerably higher incidence has been suggested, with one study finding that 76 per cent of girls aged 12–18 had been sent unsolicited nude images of boys or men (Ringrose, 2020). Data from police reports also show that the majority of those reporting cyberflashing are women under 30, and that while still the 'tip of the iceberg', reports are increasing (Bowden, 2020; Gallagher, 2020).

Collectively, these figures demonstrate that cyberflashing is commonplace, particularly for young women and girls, where the research consistently finds that approximately half or more of young women have received unsolicited penis images. Moreover, it is possible that prevalence has increased further since the COVID-19 pandemic began, with one study finding that online abuse in general has risen considerably in this time, with black and minoritised women particularly affected (Glitch UK and EVAW, 2020). This is supported by research which found that the overwhelming majority (83 per cent) of those affected by online abuse at work, including cyberflashing, said it had escalated since the pandemic began (Suzy Lamplugh Trust, 2020). Another recent survey found that men were more likely to send penis images than they were before the pandemic, though it was unclear whether this included unsolicited images (Tomchak, 2020).

This data on cyberflashing mirrors research regarding online sexual harassment more generally which finds that women are disproportionately targeted (Powell and Henry 2017, 156). While Powell and Henry found that almost one third of both women and men had received unwanted sexually explicit images, comments or emails (the most common form of online sexual harassment) the context, and consequently the impacts, varied considerably by gender (Powell and Henry, 2017, 165–166). For example, men reported receiving generic pornographic material, including advertising and spam emails, while women were more likely to receive targeted personal communications featuring unsolicited sexually explicit images (cyberflashing) and personal sexual requests (Powell and Henry, 2017, 166).

Differing experiences were also were found in the study by Gamez-Gaudix et al (2015) which discovered that online sexual victimisation was more common among women and LGBTQI+ populations than among heterosexual men. Indeed, Marcotte et al (2020) found that men identifying as gay or bisexual experienced similar rates of cyberflashing to women, though there were marked differences in men's reactions relative to women. Therefore, while women in general are particularly affected by online abuse and cyberflashing, there are differences between and among women which mean that some are targeted more than others, particularly younger and/ or black and minoritised women, and may face differing levels of recognition for the harms they experience. This intersectional context is vital to understanding the prevalence and experience of online abuse and cyberflashing (Lumsden and Harmer, 2019; Harris and Vitis, 2020).

What is cyberflashing?

While cyberflashing is one 'act' – the sending of a penis image without consent – examining victim-survivors experiences makes it clear that there is a broad spectrum of contexts in which this phenomenon arises. It involves individual acts of sexual exposure, or it can be part of a course of abusive conduct, including in harassing, stalking and grooming contexts. It can involve single or multiple pictures and videos, including acts of masturbation. Listening to women's accounts, we learn that these images are sometimes sent together with threatening or abusive dialogue or imagery. Perpetrators are strangers, daters, potential employers, colleagues, friends. Women also talk about cyberflashing taking place across all these contexts in their lives – regularly talking about multiple, even routine occurrences. These experiences demonstrate that technology collapses spaces and contexts; it is borderless and not bound to any particular location. This 'spacelessness', combined with the speed and ease with which penis images can now be shared, means that women can be exposed to abuse anywhere and any time they use digital media or a technological device (Harris and Vitis, 2020). Across all these varied contexts, there are some common elements to many women's experiences of cyberflashing, particularly its gendered nature, with the perpetrators being men, and often acting where their masculinity may have been threatened or diminished. The behaviours are sexualised in several ways: the images are sexual, and the practices often take place in the context of other forms of sexualised threats, sexual harassment or abuse.

It is important to recognise the breadth of contexts in which this abuse takes place, in order to better understand its nature, significance and impacts. Accordingly, in the following sections we explore some of the key contexts in which cyberflashing takes place, namely in public and particularly on public transport, in dating and hook-up environments, and in online and social media interactions more generally.

Cyberflashing in public spaces and on public transport

Victim-survivor testimonies reveal that women frequently experience cyberflashing in physical public spaces; in supermarkets, libraries, restaurants, museums, university campuses, airports, as well as on various forms of public transport (Gallagher, 2019f). In many of these circumstances, unknown men send penis images to women's mobile phones through the use of technology such as AirDrop and Bluetooth which enables the fast and easy distribution of material to devices close by (around nine meters). In many respects, therefore, this form of cyberflashing closely parallels physical 'flashing' – typically, when an unknown man commits sexual exposure by displaying his penis to others physically nearby (Thompson, 2016; Hayes and Dragiewicz, 2018). As Joanna, for example, explained:

> I was sitting at a bus stop … It was about midnight, I'd just been watching an Instagram story … when this dick popped up on my screen out of nowhere … Suddenly I found myself looking around … I got this creeping feeling that I was being watched, though I couldn't see anyone.
>
> (Beaty, 2019)

Rachel's experience is similar:

> I was travelling home alone by bus when a dick pic popped up on my phone. In the space of a second or two I was confused, shocked, then disgusted. But once I deleted it, I was suspicious about who'd sent it. No one I could see looked likely so I wondered if it was a joke … It didn't occur to me until afterwards that someone would deliberately send that to a stranger.
>
> (Gil, 2019)

Some women describe being sent multiple images, sometimes hundreds, by the perpetrator, even after they 'declined' the initial images, making clear they were unwanted (Gallagher, 2019a). Tara Jane, for example, described how she quickly declined a penis image she was sent on the underground, but: 'Then it popped up again, and again. So I started to go into my settings but the fucking photo kept popping up until I finally switched AirDrop off … I couldn't work out who did it – the Tube was relatively packed and it was just really grim' (Thompson, 2019).

In other examples, the penis images have been sent together with other disturbing pictures, creating an unequivocally sinister or threatening subtext, such as where 16-year-old Ursula was AirDropped a penis image alongside pictures of rotting rats while on a school trip to a museum (Precel, 2019). Some women have experienced being cyberflashed in public spaces on multiple occasions. Lisa, for example, experienced it three times at the same Tube station, convincing her that someone was spending extended periods of time there to specifically victimise women (Gallagher, 2019a). Sophie had similar experiences:

> I've been sent dick pics … on multiple occasions … including while on the subway, in a Starbucks, and at the airport. Most times, it seems like the sender targets any/ every female with their AirDrop turned on. As soon as I receive one, I see multiple other women look up from their phones just as confused as I am.
>
> (Palermino, 2018)

While Sophie's experience was of a perpetrator sending penis images to many women, in other accounts the cyberflashing is more targeted (Gallagher, 2019d). Chloe, for example, was sent multiple penis images, along with a photograph that the cyberflasher had clandestinely taken of her on the train, with a super-imposed circle drawn around her head to clearly single her out (Gallagher, 2018e). Although the perpetrator in Chloe's case remained anonymous, in other examples victim-survivors were clearly able to identify the person who had sent the images, and were even approached by them (Palermino, 2018). In one case, the victim-survivor was alone at a train station when she was approached by an unknown man, who stood close by and watched her as he clearly sent her the cyberflashing images: 'He made eye contact with me. I looked at his hands and they were shaking; his thumbs hovered over his phone waiting for my reaction. The man was so close to me. It was so intimidating' (Gallagher, 2019f). Subsequently, the man followed her until she made it to her train: 'I saw him across the concourse, staring right at me. I was being targeted, and it felt very personal' (Gallagher, 2019f).

Cyberflashing in online dating and hook-up apps

Cyberflashing is also documented as being a common experience on dating and 'hook-up' websites and apps, often characterised as being 'transactionally' inspired or as a 'clumsy' sexual engagement (Waling and Pym, 2017). However, women's testimonies demonstrate that the picture is not straightforward, and the situation is more complex. Most striking is how cyberflashing has become a routine experience for women on dating apps. As Francesca states: 'It's such a prominent thing in the world of modern dating … It's become the norm' (Perry, 2019). Cara similarly describes how she has been subject to cyberflashing 'countless' times:

> I couldn't even tell you how many times I've been sent dick pics on dating apps … without me asking. They've always been sent randomly and out of nowhere. Guys will start off seeming mega chilled, we'll be having a good chit-chat about work and life, and then you get a message which is an instant red flag, like 'So, what are your kinks? When was the last time you got laid?' and then, BAM, a penis is thrust into my inbox.
>
> (Gil, 2019)

Here Cara evocatively uses the words 'BAM' and 'thrust' to emphasise her experience of cyberflashing, as something unexpected, disruptive and forceful. In other examples, men send unsolicited penis images on dating apps without any prior contact with the victim-survivors (Johnson, 2018) or use their penis as their profile picture, unavoidably exposing women to these images as they swipe through the list of potential contacts (Gallagher, 2018e). As Rosie's experience demonstrates, and in parallel to the AirDrop examples, perpetrators of cyberflashing have continued to send penis images, despite women making it clear they were unwanted:

> [The video] was from a guy I'd been chatting to for a few days after meeting him on the dating app … It was a clip of him masturbating … I decided to send a message saying I didn't appreciate the video and then simply ignore him. However, the next day I woke to another pic, this time of him lying in bed naked with an erection … that day he sent five more messages … Each time my phone pinged I felt increasingly uncomfortable, and eventually that evening I messaged him again to say I really wasn't interested and to leave me alone, to which he responded with another obscene video of him masturbating.
>
> (Gizauskas, 2018)

In other examples, the cyberflashing has followed the victim-survivor rejecting the perpetrator's advances, with one woman reporting being bombarded with unsolicited penis images, phone calls, and explicit messages by a man up to a year after she declined to go on a second date with him (Gallagher, 2017; Amunsden, 2020). In another case, a man sent a woman a picture of an erection alongside the blade of a kitchen knife after she declined his expressed interest (Thompson, 2016). As Thompson writes of this example, the image subtext is of the 'penis as a weapon, with the ability to hurt or "punish" this woman for her apparent "transgression" by rejecting him' (Thompson, 2016). In other cases, cyberflashing occurred alongside explicit rape threats and cyberstalking, as Emmie's online dating experience demonstrates:

> After we exchanged a few messages ... I began to ignore his messages, hoping he would take the hint. Out of nowhere, he sent me a picture of his penis. I was really shocked as I'd never known anyone to do anything like that ... Over the next few days, [he] sent more images along with a message saying I 'wanted it' and that he was 'going to give it to me'. Then he began to send more messages threatening to track me down and rape me.
>
> (Gizauskas, 2018)

After Emmie blocked the man on the dating app, he proceeded to cyberstalk her and continued to cyberflash and threaten her through her personal social media accounts.

Unsolicited penis images are also described as being prevalent within certain 'hook-up' and dating apps used particularly by same-sex attracted men (Paasonen et al, 2019). However, in contrast to heterosexual dating contexts, unsolicited penis images in these contexts are commonly viewed more positively (Tziallas, 2015; Marcotte et al, 2020), or as an 'accepted actor' within this sexual infrastructure (Paasonen et al, 2019, 6; Mandau, 2020). This is attributed to penis images being a 'central feature and enabler of digitally mediated sexual cultures' among same-sex attracted men (Paasonen et al, 2019, 6). Paasonen et al (2019), for example, reference hook-up sites for men who have sex with men where profile templates explicitly encouraged users to include penis images, and where identifying photos of profile users would be limited for privacy and security reasons, meaning that it was common practice to use a penis as a profile picture. More recently, there are still many public accounts which reference the prevalence and normalcy of unsolicited penis images in same-sex social media applications (Dawson, 2019). As we discuss in the following chapter, across any context, the experience and harms of cyberflashing are non-prescriptive. In particular, we suggest the sending of unsolicited penis images in dating and hook-up contexts among men who have sex with men requires distinct consideration and analysis, due to the particular significance of these practices and connection with sexual and techno-cultures.

Cyberflashing on social media and other digital technologies

Beyond online dating contexts, cyberflashing is also regularly experienced by women engaging with social media and other online technologies, in personal and professional capacities. As with other cyberflashing contexts, sometimes the penis images are accompanied by sexually violent or abusive text (Gallagher, 2019g). In some of these cases, the perpetrators were previously known to the women, emphasising that cyberflashing contexts extend beyond strangers (Gallagher, 2019g). Melanie, for example, was sent an unsolicited penis image 'out of the blue' on Facebook, by an estranged family friend (Gallagher, 2019g). There are also examples where women have been cyberflashed by men they had only briefly interacted with, for example after attending a job interview (Gallagher, 2017). Amy, for example, received a Facebook message containing a naked full-frontal photo of a man who had interviewed her for a job days earlier, but she had heard nothing back from him (Gallagher, 2019g). Although Amy ignored the man, he continued to send images for a time afterwards.

Nonetheless, most public testimonies involve unknown men, often specifically targeting young women and girls, such as this girl describing her first experience of cyberflashing: 'I am 12 and … I wanted to get online and chat to people since my friends had done it and told me it would be fun … Then men started sending dick pics' (Press Association, 2020). This echoes Lisa's experience who, at 15, had been sent unsolicited penis images 'hundreds of times' by unknown men via social media, and had also been targeted by a man who video-called her to live-stream himself masturbating (Gallagher, 2019c). In other examples, cyberflashing is perpetrated in the context of grooming behaviours and sexual exploitation, as Mared, who was 14 at the time, describes: 'It went from "you're very pretty" and "that picture you posted is very nice" to "you've got a nice figure", then the sexual [penis] images came … I later realised how predatory it was' (Gallagher, 2019c).

There are also numerous cyberflashing testimonies from women working across a wide range of employment sectors, paralleling research documenting the widespread sexual harassment of women in work contexts (Powell and Henry, 2017; Harris and Vitis, 2020). Journalist Rosalie, for example, was cyberflashed after tweeting a call-out to local residents regarding a possible article. As she explained, a man asked to message her on Twitter: 'It seemed fairly innocuous and from a local resident, so I thought nothing of it … I asked – "Hey, did you switch to [a new energy company]?" He replied, "nope" … and then proceeded to send me three different videos, one right after the other, of him masturbating and ejaculating' (Gallagher, 2018e).

Similar to the public and the online dating contexts, women's testimonies demonstrate that cyberflashing in digital professional contexts is alarmingly commonplace – to the extent that some view receiving unsolicited penis images as an 'inevitable' occupational hazard (Dawson, 2019). As Carolanne explains regarding the Twitter account she manages at work: 'It happens so often in fact … I know so many other people who have had the exact same thing happen to them' (Gallagher, 2019a).

Finally, an emerging context in which cyberflashing occurs is via online video conferencing tools which have rapidly increased in usage following the shift to online working during the COVID-19 pandemic. Accordingly, terms such as 'zoomflashing' and 'zoombombing' have come to the fore, which refer to cyberflashers infiltrating Zoom calls or similar online meetings, and exposing themselves, or flashing unwanted penis or other pornographic images onscreen

(BBC News, 2020; Meineck, 2020; Wildmoon, 2020). These examples demonstrate that, as technology evolves and its usage changes, so will the practices of cyberflashers who will continue to find new ways to perpetrate abuse.

Why do men send unsolicited penis images?

In light of the pervasiveness of cyberflashing, and the differing contexts within which it is perpetrated, researchers and victim-survivors alike have questioned the motivations of those who perpetrate this abuse. Understanding men's motivations is essential for prevention and education initiatives, as well as law reform strategies. As we discuss in the chapters that follow, many cyberflashing laws require proof of specific motives, with the risk that only some forms of abuse are captured by the criminal law. It is welcome, therefore, that the evidence base on perpetrator motivations is growing (for example Mandau, 2020; Oswald et al, 2020).

While not encompassing all cyberflashing practices or perpetrators, these studies and perpetrator accounts provide valuable insights into the thinking of those who send unsolicited penis images. In addition, we must also be conscious of the potential weaknesses of using self-reported data from men who commit cyberflashing, given that we know in the context of other forms of sexual violence that perpetrators attempt to use 'techniques of neutralisation' (Sykes and Matza, 1957) to minimise or excuse their behaviours. With these caveats in mind, we draw out some key themes. Most importantly, and not surprisingly, motivations are not easy to separate; they are overlapping, interlocking and complex. Nevertheless, we identify here four main themes: 'transactional' motivations; sexual gratification and exhibitionism; threatening, harassing and causing distress; and we suggest that underpinning all these motivations are ideals of hegemonic masculine entitlement, power and control.

Cyberflashing as 'transactionally' motivated

Perhaps the most common framing of cyberflashing, certainly in online dating and sexting contexts, depicts men's behaviour as being 'transactionally' motivated; underpinned by the hope that sending an unsolicited penis image will result in sexual images in return, or instigate sexual activity (Ley, 2016; Salter, 2016; Waling and Pym, 2017; Mandau, 2020). These were the most common motivations reported by men in the study by Oswald et al (2020), where approximately half of men said they were motivated at least in part by the hope of receiving a sexual image in return, and more than a third hoped the images would facilitate an in-person sexual encounter. This aim for reciprocity reportedly rested on hope that the women recipients would feel sexual excitement (82 per cent) or attractive (50 per cent) (Oswald, et al 2020).

This parallels Mandau's (2020) research with young people, where she found boys drew on typical gendered constructions of heterosexuality to explain their sending of unsolicited penis images, perceiving this to be a way of complimenting or hooking-up with girls, or securing reciprocal nude pictures (also Ley, 2016; Salter, 2016). Ricciardelli and Adorjan (2018) similarly found sending unsolicited penis images is a commonplace and low-risk practice for boys, due to gendered expectations and sexual double standards that allow and reward 'active' expressions of male heterosexuality and desire. In this context, men's sending of unsolicited penis images is sometimes characterised as a 'numbers game', where men send images to numerous women, hoping for at least one 'receptive' or 'positive' response (Waling and Pym, 2017). For example, one perpetrator has described how, for all the times his unsolicited penis images were ignored or rebuffed, when one picture 'worked', it was worth it: 'I felt good about it, from the validation and the boost to my self-image, but also the precedent it opened. It was now OK for them to reply in kind, or to steer the conversation down more sexual routes' (Sarner, 2019).

Another suggested that if after a 'brief chat', he did not get a response, he would 'sometimes send a dick pic' on the basis that 'they have already lost interest so what do I have to lose?' (Gallagher, 2018c). Taken together, these reported motivations indicate men send unsolicited penis images for transactional sexual purposes, despite the evidence that women and girls often do not respond positively or reciprocate (Vitis and Gilmour, 2017; Waling and Pym, 2017; Ringrose and Lawrence, 2018; Mandau, 2020; Marcott et al, 2020; Oswald et al, 2020). David Ley (2016) suggests men may project their own sexual interests and desires onto women, with others noting that cyberflashing seems to be perceived by many men and boys as a normal and acceptable strategy of introduction and/or flirtation (Ricciardelli and Adorjan, 2019; Mandau, 2020; Oswald et al, 2020).

There is a risk that these interpretations feed into a construction of men as being 'clueless' about the impact of cyberflashing on women (Waling and Pym, 2017, 5). We need to be careful about taking at face value some men's justifications for cyberflashing as based on 'misunderstandings', particularly when we consider some are aware of the impact of their actions. For example, one cyberflasher explained: 'If the conversation had some potential, but was slowing down or becoming boring, I would sometimes send a dick pic. Because either they stop texting me or I get laid' (Sarner, 2019). There is an acknowledgement here that sending an unsolicited penis image might not be well received, but he is willing to take the 'risk' in case it results in a sexual encounter.

This echoes Ricciardelli and Adorjan's (2019) research with male teens which found they had some empathy regarding the negative impacts of sending unsolicited sexts, but no 'serious cogitation' of the 'long-lasting and caustic impact' upon their female peers. Other studies suggest a good level of awareness, with one finding just under half of men thought women found penis images distressing (31 per cent) (YouGov, 2018). As Waling and Pym (2017) argue, this evidence elucidates a tension, whereby the sending of unsolicited penis images is understood by some men as problematic, yet simultaneously normative (also Amundsen, 2020; Mandau, 2020).

While it is important to understand cyberflashing motivations in the context of gendered sexual norms, we must simultaneously be cautious that we do not normalise or minimise it, and thereby diminish perpetrators' culpability. Indeed, some elements of the 'transactional' discourse mirror arguments used at one time to explain, minimise and normalise the behaviours of physical 'flashers', such as the 'flasher' hoping to receive a reciprocal genital exposure, or their behaviour being an extension of 'normal' male sexuality and/or a misguided 'courtship' behaviour (McNeill, 1987, 96–98). While these claims may sound unreasonable today, they can serve to remind us of the tendency to minimise everyday sexual intrusions and abuses.

Sexual gratification and exhibitionism

Other explanations of physical flashing are more oriented towards sexual pathology: identifying 'compulsive' and/or 'abnormal' sexual arousal derived from the act of exposure as a form of exhibitionism (McNeill, 1987; Green, 2018; Hayes and Dragiewicz, 2018). Exhibitionism is predicated on the exposure of the genitals to another, commonly strangers, from which the individual gains sexual satisfaction (Green, 2018), as explained by those working with physical 'flashers':

[The] guy on the train using AirDrop is flashing in the digital age. The flasher is looking for something very particular: he is interested in the response, focused on the faces of these women – he wants to see shock and surprise, and a kind of disabling of the person he is flashing.

(Sarner, 2019)

It is such parallels which lead some to describe cyberflashing as 'digital exhibitionism' (Fight The New Drug, 2019). Indeed, approximately one quarter of Oswald et al's respondents reported that sending penis images 'turned them on' (2020). While Oswald et al argue that their findings indicate that cyberflashing is not typically motivated by sexual arousal, it still points to a significant proportion of men being so motivated. One perpetrator described this as follows: 'I'm not sure I can adequately explain why I did it … I found it so incredibly arousing that something took over me. There was no thinking. Just doing' (Gallagher, 2018c).

Further, even if there is a relatively small number of men motivated by sexual gratification, the nature of this sexual arousal is particularly disturbing. For exhibitionists, sexual gratification commonly comes as an 'expression of anger, particularly in cases involving male offenders and female victims', and the reaction of the victim is central to their excitement, especially 'heightened by the victim's fright' (Green, 2018, 207–208). As Ley (2016) explains in the context of cyberflashing, it is probable that some men similarly derive sexual pleasure from the prospect of the recipient coercively receiving the penis images, and/or from the recipient's reactions. Specifically, the fact that a woman rejects the perpetrator 'is not salient, because for many such men, it is the woman's disgust and rejection which is actually part of the turn-on' (Ley, 2016). This is echoed by Oswald et al's (2020) research, where 8 per cent of their participants reported: 'I get off on the knowledge that someone was forced to see my penis without their consent.'

This fusing of sexual arousal and non-consent is what Catharine MacKinnon (1979, 162) has called 'dominance eroticized'; where sexual harassment is not directly about men's sexual desires, but about knowing 'that they can go this far, this way, any time they wish and get away with it. The fact that they can do this seems itself to be sexually arousing.' Here MacKinnon is suggesting that, rather than viewing sexual harassment as a dysfunction such as with exhibitionism, this fusing of sexual gratification with compulsion and power underpins much of everyday gendered interactions.

In the context of cyberflashing, this means the motivation of sexual gratification interlocks with non-consent, and may not be an aberration, but rather a common aspect of some men's sexuality. Indeed, the prevalence of non-consensual material on mainstream pornography websites suggests a considerable market for sexually explicit material featuring force and coercion (McGlynn and Vera-Gray, 2018; 2019). This also ties into broader understandings of sexual offending where many motivations are recognised and, even in cases motivated by sexual gratification or access, are closely associated with beliefs relating to sexual entitlement, disregard for consent, and seeing sexual assault as a means of collective punishment of women (Fulu et al, 2013).

Threatening, harassing and causing distress

This underscores that we also need to understand cyberflashing as a behaviour sometimes intended to harm or negatively affect women (Thompson, 2016; Powell and Henry, 2017; Ringrose and Lawrence, 2018; Thompson, 2018). For example, a recent UK survey found that more than half of men expected women would find penis pictures gross (55 per cent), though more significantly 30 per cent thought they would find them distressing, and a quarter, threatening (24 per cent) (YouGov, 2018). Oswald et al (2020) found that significant numbers of cyberflashers hope to provoke negative reactions, with some hoping for shock (17 per cent), fear (15 per cent), and disgust (11 per cent). Others admitted that sending penis images gave them a feeling of control over the recipient (10 per cent), and that they liked to make people angry by sending penis images in response to a disagreement (8 per cent). A slightly smaller percentage were motivated by misogyny (6 per cent), agreeing with the statements: 'I don't like feminism and sending dick pics is a way to punish women for trying to take power away from men' and 'I feel a sense of dislike towards women and sending dick pics is satisfying' (Oswald et al, 2020).

These findings resonate with some victim-survivor experiences. Yasmin explained: 'I think it's quite an aggressive gesture ... they're more of a controlling thing, like: "you now have to look at my penis, whether you like it or not"' (Amundsen, 2020, 1). More starkly, Charlie states: 'Men know that women generally don't like unsolicited dick pics. They don't care. They have the mentality of: "If she's into it, great. If she's not, f★★k her." Since most women aren't into it, the purpose is pretty explicitly "well, f★★k her" ... It's meant to offend' (Gallagher, 2018c).

Multiple, overlapping motivations: masculinity, entitlement and control

There are, therefore, multiple motivations for sending unsoli-cited penis images which overlap, demonstrating that there will rarely be a single, clear motivation for committing this abuse. Further, underpinning these range of motivations is a sense of masculine entitlement, and desire for exercising power and control; hegemonic ideas of masculinity dominates some men's behaviours and justifies their acts of cyberflashing. In this context, we can also see cyberflashing as a form of homosocial bonding between men (Burkett, 2015) and a performance or reassertion of masculinity which establishes or consolidates men's gender identity and is thus intrinsically rewarding (Mandau, 2020).

Hayes and Dragiewicz (2018) identify masculine entitlement as a particularly important means of explaining cyberflashing, noting that research into a variety of forms of abuse and har-assment against women find entitlement to be a key feature. Entitlement can be understood as the socially constructed belief that men are entitled to sex, with Thompson suggesting that men's cyberflashing may be related to the increased rejection they experience online to which they respond using gendered and sexual aggression (Thompson, 2016; 2018). There may also be a sense of 'aggrieved entitlement', referring to the anger men experience when they are deprived of privileges they feel they deserve, or feel their cultural superiority is under threat (Hayes and Dragiewicz, 2018). This links to Oswald et al's (2020) findings: that perpetrators demonstrated higher levels of narcissism and endorsed greater benevolent and hostile sexism than their non-sending counterparts.

This complexity and variety mirrors what we know about sexual offending more generally, where the motivations are clearly complex and interconnected, and include sexual gratification, revenge and punishment, entitlement, power and control, recreation and adventure (Scully and Marolla, 1985; Mann and Hollin, 2007; Robertiello and Terry, 2007; Fulu et al, 2013). It also echoes research on image-based sexual abuse where findings suggest many differing, multifarious motives including coercion and control, misogyny and entitlement, a 'prank' and causing distress (McGlynn et al, 2019; Henry et al, 2020). In particular, the research on image-based sexual abuse identifies the key role of hegemonic masculinity, homosocial bonding and heteronormative misogyny in encouraging and facilitating these forms of abuse, with men seeking to present themselves as 'real men' by sharing images without consent (Hall and Hearn, 2017; Langlois and Slane, 2017). Similarly, March and Wagstaff (2017) found that men sending unsolicited penis images were often engaging in an 'aggressive mating strategy'.

Overall, therefore, this discussion of cyberflashing motivations identifies their complexity and interconnectedness, but also that they are underpinned by problematic constructions of masculinity. Many men are acting in a social context that encourages and validates aggressive sexual engagements and normalises many forms of non-consensual sexual activity, underscoring the gendered nature of cyberflashing.

Conceptualising cyberflashing as a sexual intrusion

So far, this chapter has identified the sexual and sexualised nature of cyberflashing, as well as the gendered nature of perpetration and victimisation. These features of cyberflashing closely associate it with other forms of online and public sexual harassment (Powell and Henry, 2017; Women and Equalities Select Committee, 2018). Therefore, characterising cyberflashing as a form of sexual harassment has benefits in that 'sexual harassment' as a phenomenon is widely understood and recognised as problematic.

However, a harassment framing suggests that the actions are always experienced as unwelcome or unwanted (Vera-Gray, 2017a). While we examine in the next chapter the potentially serious harms of cyberflashing, some victim–survivors do not experience it as 'harassment' for a range of reasons (Tziallas, 2015). Amundsen (2020, 7), for example, attributed some women's reluctance to identify their experiences of unsolicited penis images as a form of sexism to the dominance of a 'postfeminist discursive framework, foregrounding notions of individual agency, free choice and female empowerment'. Others may not so describe cyberflashing in light of what is allowed to count as 'unwanted' or 'unwelcome' in a gender order where women are socialised to accept, expect, and even desire assertive, intrusive attention from men (Vera-Gray 2017b, 7). It is also evident that some women's perceptions of, and reactions to, cyberflashing change over time, perhaps only later recognising it as abusive and harmful, such as in grooming contexts. Therefore, as with the term 'street harassment', a sexual harassment framing may pre-define experiences and behaviours in ways which may not capture all women's experiences and understandings (Vera-Gray 2016, 11).

Another approach to framing and conceptualising cyberflashing is to place it on a continuum of image-based sexual abuse which encompasses a broad range of practices including voyeurism, 'upskirting', pornographic 'deepfakes' and the non-consensual disclosure of sexual images (McGlynn et al, 2017; Hayes and Dragiewicz, 2018). As Hayes and Dragiewicz (2018) note, the concept of image-based sexual abuse has, however, tended to focus on images that are produced, distributed or threatened to be distributed without the consent of the person represented in the image. Nevertheless, we agree with Hayes and Dragiewicz (2018) that cyberflashing could be conceptualised as a form of image-based sexual abuse, conceived in its broadest terms. As previously discussed, across the range of contexts and forms of cyberflashing perpetration, cyberflashing commonly involves the gendered, sexualised abuse of another, by sharing sexual images without consent. This clearly fits within definitions of image-based sexual abuse which include the 'non-consensual creation and/or distribution of private sexual images' (McGlynn and Rackley, 2017; McGlynn et al, 2017) and 'taking, sharing or threatening to share nude or sexual images without consent' (Henry et al, 2020, 2). Moreover, one of the rationales for theorising image-based sexual abuse as a continuum is that it provides a holistic conceptual base which is flexible; it can encompass all existing, emerging and as yet unimagined abusive practices that falls within its definition (McGlynn et al, 2017).

Cyberflashing, therefore, can be both a form of sexual harassment and image-based sexual abuse, and both conceptualisations have value in helping to explain these practices. Nonetheless, we find there are distinct advantages in conceptualising cyberflashing as a form of 'sexual intrusion'. Similar framings have been discussed in the context of unsolicited penis images. Gillett (2018, 213), for example, suggests the sending of unsolicited penis images might be characterised as 'intimate intrusions' because of their intimidating and 'prying nature', and Waling and Pym (2017, 7) refer to the images as an 'unwelcome intrusion' into the receiver's 'offline personal space'. More generally, Harris and Vitis (2020) find value in framing digital violence as an 'intimate intrusion' which emphasises that these practices and harms are underscored by sex and gender inequalities.

Our conceptualisation builds on these ideas and key works theorising street harassment and other forms of sexual violations as intrusions (Stanko, 1985; 1987; 1990; Kelly, 1988; Vera-Gray, 2017a; 2018). Fiona Vera-Gray (2017a, 11) refers to men's intrusion as a deliberate act of putting oneself into a place or situation where one is uninvited, with disruptive effect. This conceptualisation has value for cyberflashing because it focuses on the deliberate action and thus the wrong of sending an unsolicited penis image – regardless of the perpetrator's motives, or the victim-survivor's response. With 'intrusion', therefore, there is no need to evidence a desire to harm or disrupt the target, the focus is on the deliberateness of the act. As Vera-Gray (2017a) emphasises, 'uninvited' is important as it affirms the power of women to choose who can enter their physical and emotional space, in what manner and on what terms. Intrusion also attends to the phenomenological experience of cyberflashing, where one's inner world is invaded or violated – intruded upon – rather than solely acted upon (Vera-Gray 2017a, 11).

We emphasise also the sexual and sexualised nature of cyberflashing, referring to it as a *sexual* intrusion. We have identified that cyberflashing often takes place in conjunction with other forms of sexualised harassment, threats, and abuse. Further, as we will suggest in the following chapter, the wrong of cyberflashing is the infringement of sexual autonomy, and victim-survivors commonly characterise their experiences of cyberflashing as one of sexual violation and/or sexual assault. Conceptualising cyberflashing as a sexual intrusion, therefore, ensures we recognise the specific nature of the intrusion. This, in turn, helps us to better understand its harms, and to develop appropriate forms of legal redress which characterise it as a form of sexual offending, and suitable prevention and education initiatives which examine sexual relations and ethics.

Cyberflashing, therefore, being understood as a form of sexual intrusion is, more broadly, a form of sexual violence. It shares particular characteristics with physical sexual exposure ('flashing') and silent/obscene phone calls, as well as forms of street harassment and other intrusions (Vera-Gray, 2017a). There are further commonalities with other forms of online abuse, such as image-based sexual abuse. Indeed, connecting all of these varied practices is that they can all be experienced as 'unwelcome intrusions into women's personal space which transform routine and/or potentially pleasurable activities (for example, a walk in the park, a quiet evening at home, a long train journey) into unpleasant, upsetting, disturbing and often threatening experiences' (Kelly, 1988, 97).

The sexual intrusion of cyberflashing, therefore, forms part of the 'continuum of sexual violence', the idea developed by Liz Kelly (1988) to explain the inter-relationships between different forms of sexual violence and to challenge the notion of a hierarchy of sexual offences. Kelly's predominant concern was to provide the conceptual tools by which women's experiences of men's violence could be better understood as they were (and still are) not reflected in the 'legal codes or analytic categories' of existing research (Kelly, 1988, 74). The continuum concept also enables women to make sense of their own experiences 'by showing how "typical" and "aberrant" male behaviour shade into one another' (Kelly, 1988, 75). These abuses share a 'common character' which Kelly identified as the 'abuse, intimidation, coercion, intrusion, threat and force' used to control (predominantly) women (Kelly, 1988, 76). We can see these features in many experiences of cyberflashing, as well as recognising that women's experiences do not (currently) fit within existing legal paradigms. Understanding abuse on a continuum also means that the seriousness or extent of harm cannot be inferred simply by the form or context of violence, as we discuss further in the next chapter. The different contexts for cyberflashing outlined in this chapter, therefore, should not be understood as ranked in order of seriousness (with cyberflashing on a dating app for example being 'less serious' than that experienced from a stranger on public transport).

Nonetheless, identifying 'common characteristics' must not be at the expense of recognising, and acting on, the differential experiences of differently situated women. This has been clearly articulated by Fiona Vera-Gray (2017b, 128) who comments this understanding requires us to recognise that 'although all women and girls are in some way subject to gender discrimination, all women and girls are not discriminated against in the same way'. She continues that 'hierarchies of worth' situate women and girls in relation to each other, as well as in relation to men and boys, and that we need to be attentive to how these 'hierarchical structures interact and intersect with gender inequality, and how its manifestation differs according to other markers of a woman's or a girl's social location'. This is vital not just in the development of conceptual analyses relating to violence against women (Choudhry, 2016), but also for subsequent policy development (Strid et al, 2013). In the cyberflashing and online abuse context, for example, this mandates that we understand how women are differently affected by these practices, such as the higher rates of victimisation for black and minoritised women (Glitch and EVAW, 2020).

Conclusions

It is vital that we understand cyberflashing as taking place in a variety of contexts, albeit with a shared common core of men sending penis images to another without consent. Our focus on men's sending of images to women has highlighted the gendered and sexualised nature of these practices, as well as the complexity and interlocking nature of motivations for perpetration. We have also emphasised how we need to understand cyberflashing in the context of hegemonic masculinity, where men are encouraged and often rewarded for aggressive and non-consensual sexual practices. It is in such a context that we can understand men's 'intimate intrusions'

(Stanko, 1985, 9) as unexceptional, and how such disruptions 'take on an illusion of normality, ordinariness' (Harris and Vitis, 2020, 327). This helps us to recognise the commonality of cyberflashing and how many in society act to minimise and trivialise it. Our conceptualisation of cyberflashing as a sexual intrusion that sits on a continuum of sexual violence is developed in the following chapter which examines in more detail the varied harms of cyberflashing.

TWO

The Harms of Cyberflashing

I was terrified as to who was watching me, and knowing there was a sexual predator within a few metres ... I actually called a friend while I was getting off the train and walking to my car so I wasn't alone ... On the way to my car, I was 100 per cent terrified. What if this person is following me?

(Leecie, quoted in Precel, 2019)

Cyberflashing is often trivialised and normalised, framed as a routine and unavoidable part of women's lives. However, cyberflashing is not inevitable, and its seriousness – the wrong it entails, the significant impacts it can cause – should not be minimised. Accordingly, this chapter explores the harms of cyberflashing, challenging the assumption that its impacts are less 'real' or serious simply because the image is sent digitally rather than seeing a 'flasher' in 'real life'. We examine the 'real world' harms experienced and described by victim-survivors, drawing on a wide range of publicly available testimonies and the studies that have begun to investigate this area (Amundsen, 2020; Mandau, 2020; Marcotte et al, 2020; Johansen and Tjornhoj-Thomsen, nd). Overall, it is imperative that the nature and extent of the harms of cyberflashing be properly recognised and understood, if we are to generate effective and long-lasting change through targeted prevention and education initiatives, as well as meaningful law reform.

The chapter begins by underlining that the harms of cyberflashing must be understood as gendered, as well as intersectional and contingent. We then outline that, fundamentally, cyberflashing is an infringement of sexual autonomy. Next, we explain cyberflashing as constituting an intrusive sexual violation for some, followed by considering how for others the harm manifests as humiliation. The fear and threat sometimes induced by cyberflashing is then discussed, including the similarities between physical sexual exposure, silent/obscene phone calls and cyberflashing. We also make clear the extent of the cumulative harms of cyberflashing, impacting on women's sense of safety, freedom, participation in public spaces (both online and offline) and 'right to everyday life' (Beebeejaun, 2017); all of which perpetuates and extends gender inequality. Finally, we reflect on the broader social harms of cyberflashing and how its prevalence ultimately deprives us all of a richer, more diverse public and online discourse (Citron, 2014).

Harms as gendered, intersectional and contextual

It is important to recognise at the outset that the harms of cyberflashing are deeply gendered. Most obviously, women, and young women in particular, are predominantly the targets. In addition, the sexualised form and manner of this abuse, experienced in the context of sexual violence and online sexual harassment, shape the ways in which women experience cyberflashing. Thus, cyberflashing is socially constructed, premised on gendered cultural values, attitudes and practices that are amenable to change.

Our focus is primarily on women's experiences of men sending unsolicited penis images, but it is important to highlight differences between men and women's experiences. Certainly, research by Marcotte et al (2020) on cyberflashing found that although women and men identifying as gay and/ or bisexual reported similar rates of victimisation, there were marked differences in reactions. Women reported 'overwhelmingly negative responses', with gay and bisexual men being significantly more likely to report positive responses, such as being 'entertained', 'aroused' or 'curious' (Marcotte et al, 2020). The authors suggest the different gendered responses are in part connected to dominant constructions of gender; citing, for example, contexts of hegemonic masculinity, wherein men are expected to be sexually aggressive, as well as normative constructions of femininity which idealise passivity and delegitimises women's expressions of sexual pleasure (Marcotte et al, 2020; also Salter, 2016). However, Marcotte et al (2020) also suggest that women's negative experiences are best understood as embedded within the broader heteronormative context of men's widespread sexual violence against women, which might be of less direct relevance to the experiences of men, including male sexual minorities.

While we identify in this chapter the varying harms experienced by women who have experienced cyberflashing, it is important to re-emphasise that these harms are situated, interconnected, fluid and are experienced differently by individual victim-survivors depending on their particular context. This context and variability are key to understanding sexual violence as being experienced as a continuum, without creating a hierarchy of harms (Kelly, 1988). Further, our discussion of the potentially significant harms of cyberflashing does not infer an essentialist way of understanding or experiencing this abuse. Rather, we emphasise the fluidity of such experiences across time and space, and the ways they are both connected to, and distinct from, other forms of sexual violence and inequality. We are also keenly aware of the risk that in seeking to emphasise and gain recognition for particular understandings of harm, we may reify particular experiences (McGlynn et al, 2020). This can risk new ways of 'othering, stigmatizing, violating' those who have experienced sexual violence (Gavey and Schmidt, 2011, 452). Therefore, it is important to emphasise the experiential, contingent and intersectional nature of the harms we describe. Finally, it is also vital to recognise that any harms experienced will vary in terms of their nature and consequences across, and at the intersections of, gender, race, ethnicity, sexuality, age, class and other social, political and cultural positions, with further research being required to investigate these differences in more detail in the context of cyberflashing.

Infringing sexual autonomy

At its core, cyberflashing is non-consensual sexual conduct which breaches an individual's right to sexual autonomy, as expressed so clearly by Whitney:

> It just came into my inbox and … I had no control over that happening … I felt kind of shocked and like disgusted by it … it was quite violating of my personal space and privacy. So, I didn't feel like I had an awful lot of autonomy in terms of dealing with the invasion.
>
> (Amundsen, 2020, 6)

Cyberflashing denies an individual the ability to choose whether or when they view a penis image. Importantly, though some forms of cyberflashing take place in public, the image is received on a private device, commonly a mobile phone, with which many users have a very personal relationship. Victim-survivors have thus described experiencing cyberflashing as an 'invasion' of their personal space (Gallagher, 2018a). The significance of being unable to control what comes into their personal space through their private devices is emphasised here by both Imogen and Louise:

> If you don't know what's coming when you're opening a message and it's like a sexual image, it's kind of invasive. It's like; 'I don't wanna see this. I didn't choose to see this. I didn't consent to this' … I don't think it's OK to send unsolicited like sexual anything, like sexual messages, sexual images to, especially to strangers, but kind of to anyone.
>
> (Amundsen, 2020, 7)

> When they kept sending it over and over every time I rejected it, it felt almost threatening – like they knew I was trying to stop it and were showing I had no control over it.
>
> (Gallagher, 2019b)

Accordingly, as with other forms of image-based sexual abuse (McGlynn et al, 2020), it is important to recognise that all instances of sending unsolicited penis images constitute wrongful conduct because it infringes a person's rights to sexual autonomy, integrity and privacy. This is the case regardless of the nature and extent of any further consequential harm, if any, or whether or not the action is actually welcomed by the recipient: it remains a breach of fundamental rights.

Sexual violation

Beyond the breach of sexual autonomy, some victim–survivors have described their experiences of cyberflashing in terms of violation, describing how they felt 'utterly violated', 'really violated', 'incredibly violated' (Gallagher, 2019a). As Amy explained: 'at its core, it's very invasive'; echoed by Kasia: 'I just felt totally violated' (Gallagher, 2019a). This sense of violation is commonly described, with Marcotte et al (2020) finding that almost one third of women reported feeling 'violated' after being sent unsolicited penis images. Women have particularly emphasised the sexual nature of the violation, as Lorraine explained after she received multiple penis images sent to her phone without her consent and while travelling by train: 'I felt violated, it was a very unpleasant thing to have forced upon my screen … The images were of a sexual nature and it was distressing' (Bell, 2015). Agnete explains that cyberflashing is 'not something you wanted or something that you expected' and therefore 'that's why it feels like a violation' (Johansen and Tjornhoj-Thomsen, nd).

The nature and extent of the violation of cyberflashing often goes unrecognised. This may be due to the flawed assumption that because the penis images are sent digitally, cyberflashing is therefore less 'real' or 'serious' than physical flashing, or other forms of sexual harassment and abuse. However, such a presumption overlooks the proliferation and centrality of technology in our contemporary everyday lives (Powell and Henry, 2017). Increasingly the digital lives we lead can be understood as being constitutive of who we are and our lived experiences in the world (Arnold, 2003; Miller, 2014).

As a result, personal devices such as smartphones are now understood as being highly 'intimate' technologies which complicate the supposedly clear demarcation between online and offline worlds (Henry and Powell, 2015; Harris and Vitis, 2020). Such technologies, therefore, must now be recognised as deeply intertwined with our understanding of who we are, our relationship with the world, and our sense of relatedness and community (Arnold, 2003; Miller, 2014). With continued use, these technologies also come to be experienced as extensions of ourselves and our corporeal bodily awareness (Turkle, 2007; Park and Kaye, 2018; Mandau, 2020). Ultimately, we are at the stage whereby there is an almost irreducible relationship between these intimate technologies and our being in the world (Richardson, 2012).

The intrusion of cyberflashing, therefore, constitutes an invasion of victim–survivors' very personal space and inner-world. Jess expressed this well when she said: 'I think our phones are actually a very personal and intimate belonging … and it felt like my phone was infected' (Gallagher, 2018e). Cyberflashing is experienced in, and intrudes upon, the real physical world, not some separate 'virtual' online space. This is clearly conveyed by Charlotte when describing her experience of being Airdropped an unsolicited penis image on public transport:

> I took out my phone and started reading ... when a picture popped up on the screen. It was a penis. Flaccid. Hairy. Poorly lit. Underneath the full screen high-resolution dick pic were two options – 'accept' or 'decline'. Ha. As if I had been given the choice ... With harassment, it's rare for someone else to see it, and even rarer for someone to speak up. Now it had happened on my most personal device ... I hit DECLINE. It was gone ... The [perpetrator's] intent, however, had been accomplished. I'd seen it. I'd become upset. He had stolen my attention and time and managed, somehow, to make me feel ashamed.
>
> (Palermino, 2018)

Charlotte describes her intimate relationship with her mobile phone, as her most 'personal device', and emphasises the non-consensual nature of the intrusion which 'stole' her attention and time. Anne is similar in her description, talking about how sexual exposure has moved online and that while 'a flasher still attacks you in a public place' it is now 'through your most trusted, indispensable device: your phone' (Branigin, 2016). This removal of barriers between physical and online spaces and experience is expressed by Frederikke when she talked about how a conversation can be perfectly normal and 'then there's this penis right in your face' (Johansen and Tjornhoj-Thomsen, nd).

This violation is heightened by the sexual dimension of cyberflashing. Women have stressed this side of the experience, characterising the penis images as unequivocally 'sexual' (Dean, 2015); the sender as a 'sexual predator' (Precel, 2019); and their experience of cyberflashing as a form of sexual assault (Beattie, 2018). Others have used terms associated with other forms of sexual violence, speaking of the experience using words like 'thrusting' (Branigin, 2016), 'forcefulness' (Bell, 2015) and 'bombardment' (Gallagher, 2019c). As one victim–survivor stated: 'I felt super violated. It's a way of assaulting somebody without touching, of getting into my personal space without getting close' (Beattie, 2018). Rochelle, who was AirDropped an unsolicited penis image on the Underground, explained: 'It seems predatory to me because it's subjecting people to unwanted and inappropriate images' (Gil, 2019).

This sexual dimension of cyberflashing results in the sexual nature of its harms. Jenna characterises this well: 'It seems almost silly and petty, but at the same time, it was a huge invasion of privacy ... I felt dirty. It's not like someone actually grabbed me or touched me, but it's in my head' (Kurzius, 2019). Jenna acknowledges the common trivialisation of cyberflashing but simultaneously draws on vocabulary of feeling consequentially 'dirty' or 'polluted', common frames of reference used by victim-survivors of sexual abuse to describe a lingering sense of sexual harm (Fairbrother and Rachman, 2004). This also echoes the earlier comment from Jess feeling as though her phone was 'infected' (Gallagher, 2018e).

These experiences underscore the sexual nature of both the cyberflashing offending and its harms. Central to this is the symbolic and experiential significance of cyberflashing: it constitutes a sexual intrusion which violates a person's personal, embodied space, and which is perpetrated *with a penis*. Therefore, we suggest that the interconnection of cyberflashing to broader patterns of men's sexual violence against women must not be understated. Accordingly, some victim-survivors have explicitly compared cyberflashing to the threat of rape, as Justina who was sent an unsolicited penis image on public transport reflected: '[Cyberflashing] is another example of women not being equal to men in public spaces ... we can't walk home alone at night without fear of being raped ... and now they're getting into our phones too' (Gallagher, 2019a).

These experiences and harms, therefore, are necessarily connected to the unsolicited images being of penises, rather than other sexual organs or sexualised body parts, because of the centrality of the penis to acts of rape and sexual assault (although there is debate in this area, see McKeever, 2019). This is not to say that the penis is inherently threatening in image or form. As Paasonen et al (2019, 2: also Hayes and Dragiewicz, 2018) argue, penis images, like penises, are multivalent objects which 'move in and across different frames of interpretation shaped by the affective registers of, for instance, shame, desire, disgust, interest, amusement and aggression'. However, as the authors also note, when deployed in a context of non-consent, penis images function as a figure of phallic power, imbued with gendered heterosexual dynamics of male sexual aggression, and a fundamental lack of sexual safety commonly experienced by women (Paasonen et al, 2019, 2).

Humiliation

Closely related to experiencing cyberflashing as a sexual violation is the sense of humiliation and shame that it can engender. Janay, who was cyberflashed while travelling to work, describes the 'heatwave of embarrassment' she felt: 'The truth is, no matter how strong I thought I was, he turned me, with a picture, into a weak person, feeling humiliated and with no ability to stand up for myself … the incident still repeats in my mind' (Boulos, 2019). This feeling of acute humiliation is shared by others, with Amy talking about how she was 'so embarrassed' (Gallagher, 2019a), and 16-year-old Ursula describing how she was 'embarrassed' and 'disturbed' at receiving the unsolicited image while on a school trip (Precel, 2019). Other women describe feeling demeaned and humiliated, with Natalie saying she was 'mostly shocked and disgusted as well as embarrassed'; Suzy 'felt frightened, ashamed, confused'; Beth was 'utterly horrified'; Ellie stated: 'It's so horrible and made me feel really uncomfortable' (Gallagher, 2019a). We can see that this sense of humiliation is also connected to the feelings of sexual violation discussed in this chapter where victim-survivors refer to feeling 'dirty'.

Humiliation can also be understood as infringing the dignity of the person, a concept which emphasises the worth of all individuals: all are deserving of respectful treatment, to be treated as ends and not means (Gillespie, 2019). In this way, an individual's dignity is 'dishonoured through a failure to show respect, through the treatment of others as less than creatures of inherent worth' (Reaume, 2003, 31–32). This resonates with those who have experienced cyberflashing, revealing another layer of harm. As Johansen and Tjornhoj-Thomsen (nd) describe, cyberflashing demonstrates a 'lack of care for the other person's agency and consent', adversely impacting on individuals' 'embodied sense of dignity'.

Furthermore, although there is little research on experiences of being sent unsolicited penis images with trans or other gender diverse individuals (Waling and Pym, 2017), there are publicly available examples explaining that unsolicited penis images can be experienced as disrespectful. Actor Mya Taylor, for example, has commented that, like many trans women on social media, she receives a 'steady stream' of unsolicited penis images from men who, she interprets, sexually admire trans women but do not view 'us as worthy of respect' (Lees, 2015). This re-emphasises that we must be particularly mindful of there being intersectional, conducive contexts for cyberflashing, including racism, homophobia and transphobia (Collins, 2000).

Inducing threat and fear: what might happen next?

While cyberflashing may seem like a new form of sexual intrusion, in fact it bears many similarities to age-old forms of sexual violence, particularly physical sexual exposure and silent/obscene phone calls. Recognising these connections is important to developing our understanding of the nature of the fear and threat experienced by some women, as well as the cumulative nature of the harms and how these experiences are best understood as part of a continuum of sexual violence (Kelly, 1988).

Women who have suffered cyberflashing have frequently connected their experiences to physical sexual exposure, both experientially and performatively (Thompson, 2016; Hayes and Dragiewicz, 2018). For example, Gail remarks: 'It is the same as physical exposure and it should be treated as such' (Gallagher, 2019a). Mallory makes the same link stating that: 'It's the same thing as flashing in public' (Beattie, 2018); as does Stine, saying 'it's actually kind of like a flasher' (Johansen and Tjornhoj-Thomsen, nd). Another victim-survivor, who has experienced both abuses, identified the similarities: 'both are a complete invasion of your private space, whether physically or digitally, and both forms completely blindside you and take you by surprise' (Gallagher, 2018b). As a result, victim-survivors have questioned the logic of differentiating cyberflashing from its physical counterpart, with one stating: 'I don't see how … the guard of glass on a screen differentiates the impact of a man in a mac walking down the street suddenly opening it [and] exposing himself' (Gallagher, 2019e).

When investigating physical sexual exposure, Hanmer and Saunders (1984) summed up the harms experienced by women as their 'well-founded fear' about what might happen next. Sexual exposure, they explained, 'may promote fears of injury and death to a woman' because of her 'uncertainty about what may happen next', where the 'greater the uncertainty about the outcome, the more terrifying the encounter' (Hanmer and Saunders, 1984, 33–34). As one woman straightforwardly stated: 'you wonder what he is going to do next' (McNeill, 1987, 102). Other women experience sexual exposure as a 'message from the [perpetrator] that, if he chose to, he could also rape or murder them' (Bennetto, 1995), reflecting their sense of embodied vulnerability, the 'imminent potentiality of rape' (Vera-Gray, 2017a, 89) and the anticipation of escalation to serious physical harm.

This echoes women's experiences of silent or obscene phone calls: what Carole Sheffield (1993) characterised as the 'invisible intruder'. Sheffield's research found that such calls induced significant levels of fear because of the 'concern that the call might not be random, and that the intrusion would not be limited to an obscene phone call, but would escalate to a physical assault' (Sheffield, 1993, 76). One woman described how she felt 'violated, nervous, paranoid', with another referring to how the calls 'reinforced my feelings of vulnerability, as rapable' (Sheffield, 1993, 76, 78). Liz Kelly similarly explains that such calls are 'experienced by women both as a specific form of the threat of sexual violence and as violating in themselves' (Kelly, 1988, 101). One woman explained that: 'I've received telephone calls that feel like a sexual assault' (Kelly, 1988, 101). She continued that the calls 'upset me a lot because I felt that was the ultimate invasion of my privacy for someone to phone my house' (Kelly, 1988, 102). As with cyberflashing, therefore, there is a similar sense of violation of the personal, private space of the home and phone, as well as fear of what might follow.

As Kelly argues, it was as much the uncertainty of what the call means, as the actual content, that concerned women and preoccupied them afterwards (Kelly, 1988, 102). This is important also in terms of cyberflashing. Women are not harmed simply by the existence of a penis image (though it is possible that younger girls may have a different reaction), but rather by what the image represents and what it might mean. Cyberflashing is not, therefore, about offensiveness, but about violence, threat and fear. Kelly continues that while 'flashing' and silent/obscene phone calls are 'in and of themselves violating', both rely 'in part for their impact on the explicit or implicit threat of further assault' (Kelly, 1988, 97).

What unites these experiences, and connects them to some cases of cyberflashing, is the fear and threat induced by not knowing what might happen next, in essence the fear of further sexual violence. In cases of physical sexual exposure, the reaction of women depended on their perception of the possible danger in that situation: was she alone; was she in a deserted place (McNeill, 1987, 102; Riordan, 1999). Such assessments are not possible with silent phone calls, often increasing the sense of fear and threat. Women have talked about how their fear was compounded by the unknown: did the perpetrator know them, was it random, could he see her, was he watching, is he nearby, does he know where she lives, is it going to continue (Kelly, 1988, 100).

These experiences are echoed in some women's accounts of cyberflashing. Women have recounted feeling immediately 'frightened', 'terrified', 'vulnerable' and 'exposed' by acts of cyberflashing (Gallagher, 2019a), as well as 'scared' (Gizauskas, 2018). It is, therefore, imperative we recognise that cyberflashing takes place in 'real-life', and therefore can also engender 'real-life' threats, consequences and harms. This sense of threat and fear is particularly experienced by those receiving unsolicited images from strangers in public spaces, or where victim-survivors had reason to believe the perpetrator might be located nearby. For example, Chloe was AirDropped penis images by a stranger on a train and said she felt 'vulnerable for the rest of my trip … it was scary not knowing who it was … that they might be looking at me or potentially follow me off the train' (Gallagher, 2019a).

Another woman describes similar fears: 'you've got someone here who is doing this, it could escalate' (Gallagher, 2018d); echoed by Sophie: 'As a young woman who travels up and down the country alone quite often, the idea that this, or something worse, might happen to me next time is scary' (Gallagher, 2019e). Women are also unsettled by the fact that they feel they are not supposed to have these fears, yet they do, echoing many women's experiences of street harassment (Vera-Gray, 2018). Joanna said: 'I did think that this might seem quite insignificant in the grand scheme of things. But then I reckoned: if a person feels justified in this behaviour, what else are they capable of?' (Beaty, 2019). And, as Katie describes, not knowing which man sent the penis image can extend the sense of threat to all men:

> Of course I clicked decline immediately, but that didn't stop my face flushing bright red. I sat frozen in my seat, suddenly aware of every male on the upper deck [of the bus]. Was it the old man smiling at his phone screen to my left? The chuckling teens on the back row? The builder sitting beside me?
>
> (Strick, 2019)

In this context, the unknown identity and proximity of the perpetrator makes it impossible to accurately assess the potential risk of escalation and take protective action. As Ella states: 'with cyberflashing, because you don't know who's sent it, and you're in a public space, that threat is never really eliminated' (Gallagher, 2019e). Other victim-survivors have reflected that the hidden nature of cyberflashing – its visibility often limited to the screen of the victim-survivor's personal device – makes cyberflashing feel all the more threatening and targeted:

> I felt very alone and vulnerable. Because it's not like flashing where everyone can see if it happens to you in public and might intervene or try to help. It was more internalised – no one knew what was on my phone. I was singled out, I was being targeted, and it felt very personal.
>
> (Gallagher, 2019f)

This sense of fear and threat can be intense and prolonged. On receiving a penis image, Janay says that her response was 'immediate: decline', but she continues that she 'couldn't reject the insecurity and fear it left me with' (Boulos, 2019).

We know that, in response to threats such as physical 'flashing' and street harassment, women try to assess, almost subconsciously and instantaneously, the potential for further harm (Vera-Gray, 2017a; Vera-Gray and Kelly, 2020). They are trying to work out what is the 'right amount of panic' (Vera-Gray, 2018). But, this is all the more difficult when faced with online activities and the 'skills' accumulated off-line may be of little help in these stranger–public–cyberflashing contexts. The perpetrator is not identifiable; their purpose therefore is even more difficult to discern; it is impossible to tell if you are being targeted or it's happening to others as well. Further, cyberflashing can directly disrupt women's safety strategies which can often involve looking at a mobile phone in public, deliberately to avoid eye contact or seeming open to engagement. The threatening nature of the experience is, therefore, heightened by fact that the cyberflashing disrupts the very strategy being adopted to protect oneself. And, this still leaves the major question unanswered: what next? As Joanna explains:

> With old-school flashing at least you could see that it was a pathetic old man, and you could just turn around … the [penis image] I got is clearly a young man so I couldn't be as confident I could escape or take him on, and I was alone at the bus stop. I assumed he was watching me, which was the creepy thing. Walking home I was thinking, 'Is he following me?'
>
> (Strick, 2020)

Hayes and Dragiewicz (2018) also point out that while receiving unsolicited penis images online may seem less disturbing than physical sexual exposure because the sender may not be physically present, they still may know or access personal information about the victim-survivor. Many dating apps and other social media have settings which provide information about the recipient's location, and others require users' real names, meaning the sender may be able to identify the victim and potentially where they live and work (Hayes and Dragiewicz, 2018). Certainly victim-survivors were aware of this potential threat, as Rosie, who was cyberflashed on a dating app, explains: '[The dating app] reveals full names, so he knew my surname … From the chats we'd had, we'd realised we lived just around the corner from each other, which made me … frightened … that he might somehow track me down' (Gizauskas, 2018).

Cumulative harms and the right to 'everyday life'

As a form of sexual violence, the harms of cyberflashing must be understood as cumulative and connected to women's other experiences of harassment and abuse, which cumulatively impact adversely on women's 'right to everyday life' – the right to go about their lives without fear of harassment, abuse and other sexual intrusions (Beebeejaun, 2017). In particular, it is clear from some victim-survivors that cyberflashing is experienced as part of a wider pattern of everyday sexism and sexual violence (Hayes and Dragiewicz, 2018; Ringrose and Lawrence, 2018; Thompson, 2018). As Kate noted: 'it felt like [the cyberflashing] was another harassment women have to absorb' (Gallagher, 2018a).

Therefore, many women do not experience cyberflashing as a 'one-off' incident, but rather as another aspect of the everyday objectification, inequality and sexual double standards that women routinely navigate. This is the 'continuum of fear and threat' that Kelly identifies, and which extends from specific times or places to 'all aspects of women's daily lives' (Kelly, 1988, 97–98). It would be wrong to minimise the gruelling nature of this cumulation of women's 'routine' experiences of cyberflashing (Amundsen, 2020). As one woman stated: 'I know men think women should just deal with these types of micro-aggressions because it's not 'that bad' but it's so constant. Can't I just use Facebook or other social media without worrying this might happen?' (Gallagher, 2019a).

In this context, many women engage in 'precautionary strategies' (Stanko, 1987) and 'safety work' (Vera-Gray and Kelly, 2020), such as curtailing their use of technology and activity online, turning off Bluetooth or AirDrop, removing themselves from particular apps, or using a man's name for their phone ID (Gallagher, 2018f). As one woman explains: 'I just hate the idea of turning my AirDrop on, even momentarily, and being bombarded again. I hate that men control how I behave' (Gallagher, 2018f). This demonstrates how the pervasiveness of cyberflashing undermines women's ability to freely live their lives and exercise their citizenship in public spaces, both online and offline.

Such experiences connect with research evidencing women's experiences of online and offline spaces as inflected by the threat and fear of sexualised harassment, abuse and violence from men (Stanko, 1987; Valentine, 1989; Pain, 1993; Brison, 2003; Vera-Gray, 2017a). The sense of living in a hostile world, pervaded by the possibility of sexual violence, constraining their liberty and what has been termed their 'space for action' (Lundgren, 1998; Jeffner, 2000 cited in Vera-Gray, 2017b; Kelly, 2003). This idea focuses on how individual perpetrators, together with broader social expectations, opportunities and experiences, can constrain women's choices, options and therefore their 'space' for taking 'action' and exercising agency. It aligns with the idea of how experiencing abuse, in the context in which we live, can constrain one's 'horizons of possibility' (Vera-Gray, 2017b) by serving to limit what seems viable in a world where a pervasive sense of threat may also exist. Crucially, this notion does not erase agency, but recognises that our agency is exercised in context, what Vera-Gray (2017a) has referred to as 'situated agency'.

Importantly, this situated experience varies according to everyone's positions with intersecting axes of power and privilege. Thus, experiences of narrowed 'space for action' will differ according to each individual, being particularly felt in situations of precarity, and where multiple and interlocking oppressions and inequalities intersect. This evokes Stark's (2007) assertion that to understand harm comprehensively, we must not only look at what is 'done to' victim-survivors, but also what they are stopped from doing. Cyberflashing, therefore, can be seen as constituting a 'liberty crime' (Stark, 2007, 13) with enduring impacts which restrict a victim-survivor's 'right to everyday life' (Beebeejaun, 2017; McGlynn et al, 2020). In essence, not only are women entitled to freedom *from* being cyberflashed, but they should have freedom *to* make choices such as their right to turn on Airdrop in public without fear of harm.

Broader social and cultural harms

The detrimental effects of the prevalence and normalisation of cyberflashing resonate across society, particularly shaping cultures of non-consent around online activities generally and image-sharing in particular. Specifically, some police refer to cyberflashing as being about 'just photos' (Boulos, 2019) and victim-survivors talk of the 'normality of this sexually aggressive behaviour' (Gallagher, 2018f). As Naomi exemplifies: 'I was unsurprised and resigned to be honest. Not really shocked, just disappointed by men in general' (Gallagher, 2019a). The risk is that with the increasing commonality of cyberflashing, non-consensual sexual activity more generally is increasingly being normalised.

Thus, while individual acts of cyberflashing can themselves cause significant individual harms, the repercussions adversely impact on all members of society, including engendering a culture conducive to further sexual violence. In this way, behaviours such as cyberflashing, together with other forms of online harassment such as image-based sexual abuse, become mutually reinforcing; reproducing deeply problematic attitudes and cultures of non-consent (McGlynn and Rackley, 2017; McGlynn et al, 2020). Thus, cyberflashing may help to sustain a culture – a set of attitudes that are not universal, but which extend beyond those immediately involved as perpetrators or victim-survivors of this abuse – in which sexual consent is marginalised. And, by extension, this means that other acts of sexual violence are perhaps less likely to be recognised as such.

Beyond sexual violence, the adverse impacts can be felt in civic engagement more generally. In particular, the cumulative effect of each instance of cyberflashing, together with other forms of online abuse and harassment, contributes to a culture in which victim-survivors feel they have little option but to 'sign off' (or fail to sign on). As one victim-survivor describes: 'It makes me feel as though I should go on lockdown and shut down all my personal social media accounts, as if that's the only way to stop this happening' (Gallagher, 2019a). This is the 'silencing effect' of online abuse and harassment (Amnesty, 2017; Glitch, 2020) which inhibits women's exercise of rights to freedom of speech and participation in society (Amnesty, 2017; European Parliament, 2018). This 'silencing' not only 'solidifies male dominance of online spaces by eliminating and *muting* women's voices from the internet' (Citron, 2010, 391 emphasis in original), but also inhibits women's ability and willingness to 'participate in online life as equals' (Citron, 2010, 31). In doing so, this deprives all of society of a richer, more varied and diverse public and online discourse (Citron, 2014; Law Commission, 2020, para 4.100–4.103).

This also feeds into a broader sense of gendered inequality, as expressed by Justina: 'This is another example of women not being equal to men in public spaces' (Gallagher, 2019a). Angela agrees: 'I know men might struggle to understand why it upsets women so much ... it just is another thing that makes us feel like second class citizens. The fact that we are uncomfortable is such a secondary concern to them' (Gallagher, 2019a).

In considering online sexual harassment more broadly, Franks writes that the aggregate result of gendered online harassment is to '(re)make women into a marginalised class, using sexual objectification and gender stereotyping to make women feel unwelcome, subordinated, or altogether excluded from socially meaningful activities' (Franks, 2012, 658). This echoes research by Powell and Henry (2017, 181) which demonstrates that 'abusive online behaviours contribute to the social exclusion of women and other marginalised groups'.

Consequently, cyberflashing needs to be understood as generating significant, broader social harms – for individual women and for society as a whole. In this way, cyberflashing can be understood as a form of 'cultural harm' (McGlynn and Rackley, 2009; McGlynn and Rackley, 2017; Vera-Gray and McGlynn, 2020). It extends the sense of fear, threat and harm that women experience into all public and online spaces; it impinges upon women's civil liberties, civic participation and right to everyday life; and, therefore, it normalises and furthers gender inequality. In turn, this impacts adversely on society as a whole, normalising non-consensual sexual activity, reducing the vitality and diversity of civic and online life and perpetuating gendered patterns of interaction and inequality.

Conclusions

At its core, cyberflashing infringes an individual's right to sexual autonomy. This wrong, in and of itself, means that we must challenge cyberflashing and strive for change. But, as we have argued, cyberflashing can also induce serious harms. Drawing on testimonies from victim-survivors and emerging research in this field, we have identified five key ways of understanding these harms: as sexual violation, humiliation, threat and fear, cumulative harms, and broader societal harms. Crucially, these harms are gendered. Their impacts commonly stem from women's broader experiences of living in a society where sexual violence is commonplace, and gender continues to shape and permeate sexual and everyday relations, offline and online.

We must embrace a nuanced understanding of cyberflashing which recognises the *prima facie* wrong of the act, and its potentially serious impacts, particularly on women, while simultaneously recognising that the nature and impacts of cyberflashing may be experienced differently, by different individuals, across different groups, and in different situated contexts. We know, for example, that black and minoritised women experience higher levels of online abuse, and street harassment is experienced as forms of both racial and gender discrimination (Imkaan and EVAW, 2016; Glitch and EVAW, 2020; Thiara and Roy, 2020). Such differential impacts and interlocking experiences are also likely in cyberflashing contexts. It is vital, therefore, to recognise that any harms experienced will vary in terms of their nature and consequences across, and at the intersection of, genders, ethnicities, sexualities, age, class, disability, and any other social, political and cultural positions.

Understanding the significant nature and extent of the harms of cyberflashing is vital to a project of change generally, and to law reform in particular. Moreover, understanding the serious, cumulative nature of the harms is crucial to delineating the scope of any legislation, and for its effective implementation. It is only by meaningfully engaging with the experiences of victim-survivors, and recognising the full extent and nature of the harms of cyberflashing, that an effective and practicably enforceable law might be formulated.

PART II

Reforming the Criminal Law

THREE

Justifying Criminalisation: Recognition, Redress and Justice

The law needs to catch up. The government needs to catch up with the times and implement something that stops people thinking it's okay.

(Lisa, quoted in Gallagher, 2019e)

In her pathbreaking book *Sexual Harassment of Working Women*, Catharine MacKinnon (1979, xii) stated: 'I hope to bring to the law something of the reality of women's lives'. In doing so, she succeeded in generating public recognition of the extent and nature of sexual harassment, as well as establishing how law may provide some redress for its harms. Such a project – to demonstrate law's failures to recognise and address women's experiences, and to then reshape, revise and reform the law – has been the work of feminists, scholars, activists and lawyers over decades. Recognising that law can be a powerful agent of change, it has been harnessed to secure greater equality, liberty and freedom for women.

At the same time, law continues to be a bulwark against change. It continues to oppress, exclude and minimise claims and interests, particularly from black, minoritised and other marginalised communities and individuals. For some, therefore, engaging with law and advocating for law reform will never redress such oppressions; the solution being prison abolition and dismantling the entire edifice of law (Smith, 2010; Dixon and Lakshmi Piepzna-Samarasinha, 2020). Law, therefore, is a site of struggle: for meaning and recognition of harms and experiences, for meaningful redress, and for the multiple meanings of justice.

It is with an understanding of these tensions that this chapter considers the possibilities and limitations of turning to the criminal law. We outline our approach, identifying the need for a nuanced and complex understanding of how, when and why we should, or should not, use the criminal law. In the end, we suggest that the criminal law has a role to play in providing recognition and redress to some victim-survivors of cyberflashing, as well as supporting education and prevention measures; albeit within a framework that appreciates the considerable challenges of deploying the criminal law, not least its uneven application in practice.

Nonetheless, we wish to be clear at the outset: we are not suggesting that the criminal law should be the first, only or that it is the best means of tackling cyberflashing. It should only ever be one of many options. We conclude, therefore, that while the law should be 'neither the starting point nor the end result'; due to its power, it is an inevitable part of this struggle and 'must be addressed' (Conaghan, 1996, 431). Finally, engagement with the law is vital in the current political climate where criminal law reform is being actively considered (BBC, 2019; Law Commission, 2020). To abandon this terrain now would concede ground to what can be a powerful tool against harm and abuse. It would also risk new criminal laws being introduced that do not effectively provide recognition, redress or a sense of justice to victim-survivors of cyberflashing.

Challenging criminalisation

While law can be a powerful mechanism for challenging abuse, it is also a means of perpetrating harm. The law frequently and continuously fails to meet its loftier ambitions, particularly for women, as well as black and minoritised communities. The law discriminates, privileges, marginalises and can be an active tool in oppression. Therefore, in turning to law, we risk legitimising it, with its masculine bias and other multiple forms of oppression. This is why Smart, among others, warned feminists against fixating on law as a main site of struggle; stating that in 'accepting law's terms in order to challenge law, feminism always concedes too much' (Smart, 1989, 5). Further, the lure is often to focus on 'this' law or 'that' change, trying to fit the 'solution' into pre-existing procedures, languages, frames (Naffine, 1990). Fraser expanded this point, arguing that feminist demands can often be co-opted by neoliberal and populist movements which, in turn, deflect feminists from seeking genuine economic and systemic redistributive resolutions (Fraser, 2012).

While these concerns are true for all law, they are particularly apposite when engaging with the criminal law. Indeed, many have argued that feminists relying on the criminal law to tackle sexual violence have been co-opted by a punitive, neo-liberal state seeking to shore itself up by deploying feminist arguments for its own ends (Bernstein, 2005; 2012; Bumiller, 2008; Kim, 2018; Gruber, 2020). The result is 'decades of feminist anti-violence collaboration with the carceral state or that part of the government most associated with the institutions of police, prosecution, courts, and the system of jails, prisons, probation and parole' (Kim, 2018, 220). Kim (2018, 222) charts this rise of 'carceral feminism', arguing that characterising gender violence as a crime 'became a rallying point for feminists to fight for institutional change and to attempt to gain popular support for what was already becoming a preoccupation with crime'.

This contributed, Kim argues, to a shift from 'gender violence envisioned as a broad social and political problem, to one defined more narrowly as a crime' (Kim, 2018, 222). The result is that neoliberal governments gain political advantage through their apparent embrace of feminism (Porter, 2020), enabling them to effect penal toughness 'in a benevolent feminist guise' (Bernstein, 2012, 235). Goodmark (2018) continues that preferring a criminal justice response absolves the state from having to confront the underpinning structural situations which generate the abuse in the first place. Further, it is not only the problem of mass incarceration of black and minoritised men that has given rise to this critique, but also the criminalisation of vulnerable women, often also black and minoritised, such as through mandatory arrest policies regarding domestic abuse (Goodmark, 2011; 2018; Porter, 2020).

Black feminists in particular, therefore, have challenged criminalisation campaigning, arguing for greater understanding of the differential impacts on individuals and groups based on intersections of race, ethnicity, class, gender and other social categories (Crenshaw, 1991; Collins, 1997). In particular, the vastly differential experiences of black and other women of colour have been documented, demonstrating the 'disproportionate vulnerability to violence among marginalized women' (Kim, 2018, 224). The intersectionality critique also challenges white feminists who have 'ignored and often exacerbated the oppressive and violent conditions of women of color in the United States' (Kim, 2018, 224). There is, therefore, an urgent need to embed intersectionality in debates over the use of criminal justice processes, and in doing so to recognise the power of anti-criminalisation arguments.

Complicating criminalisation

While arguments resisting criminalisation have great force, another option is to engage critically, examining options and possibilities (Terweil, 2020). As Wegerstad (2020) argues, in considering the boundaries of criminalisation, there are a multitude of differing theories and perspectives. Each approach produces its own justifications and delineations for action, leading Lacey to argue for a more 'multi-disciplinary' criminalisation debate which considers social, economic, historical, empirical and political implications and evidence (Lacey, 2009). Too often, Lacey argues, criminalisation debates focus on single contexts or traditions, resulting in an impoverished debate. In this vein, Amy Masson (2020) calls for a greater recognition of the deeply complex nature of the state and criminal strategies, and for discussion beyond the common resort to discursive 'polarisation' and 'erasure of nuance'.

Lise Gotell (2015, 56) has similarly argued that we need to move past criminal law engagements being characterised as 'always regressive and misguided'. This chimes with Gotell's (2015, 61) specific focus on the nature of law, arguing that we need a much more nuanced understanding of it; namely recognising 'law as a dis-unified field and as a site of struggle over gender'. In other words, we must guard against any simplistic assumption that adopting a law is actually a 'victory', for penal populism, feminism or whatever group supposedly 'won'. Law develops unevenly; it is a site of change, but also of struggle and resistance. In this way, the law is 'neither a tool for the realisation of feminist goals', nor is it responsible for 'inevitably reproducing forms of domination' (Gotell, 2015, 61). Gotell (2015, 68) provides the example of the introduction of an affirmative consent standard in Canadian sexual assault laws which produced highly contradictory implications, including the decontextualising of sexual violence, but it also provided a discursive platform for a radical change to victim-blaming narratives. Thus, the law reform process is complicated: not always and inherently negative, or indeed positive.

There are examples of this more variegated approach to criminalisation within the UK; though, to be clear, it is undoubtedly the case that across the UK there are similar problems to the US in terms of high rates of imprisonment of black and minority ethnic men (Prison Reform Trust, 2019). Recent evidence in the time of COVID-19 has further demonstrated disproportionate policing of men from black and minority ethnic communities both in terms of the use of existing criminal powers, but also new pandemic-related offences (Brunt, 2020). As Marc Tran (2015, 193) considers in the context of street harassment prohibitions, such laws may enable the easier criminalisation of harassment by black men, as white men carrying out similar acts of harassment are doing so in places more hidden, in the boardrooms, schools, workplaces, where they are in positions of power and largely invisible to the police. This discriminatory impact of criminalisation can also have disparate impacts on black and minoritised women, minimising their harms, erasing their experiences, and risking over-use of the criminal law (Thiara and Gill, 2010; Uhrig, 2016; Sisters for Change, 2017; Thiara and Roy, 2020). Engaging with the criminal law, and criminal justice system, therefore, does raise similar concerns to those in the US about the potential adverse impacts on marginalised communities.

Therefore, as Day and Gill (2020) argue, an intersectional perspective must recognise that any intervention, such as criminalisation, will not be experienced by different groups in the same way. Intersectional scholars, they note, have 'warned of the dangers associated with mainstream feminism's assumption that all women face a similar risk of gendered violence and, therefore, require the same responses in practice and policy terms' (Day and Gill, 2020, 846). Day and Gill's (2020, 846) analysis shifts us away from an anti-carceral feminist analysis which precludes any interventions or partnerships with criminal justice agencies, towards one which may recognise their role, but argues for greater intersectional understanding of impacts and outcomes. It also emphasises that it is 'imperative' that a critical intersectional analysis is central to, but does not preclude, the 'introduction and evaluation of new criminal justice policies' (Day and Gill, 2020, 846). In the same spirit, a recent Imkaan report identifies that some black and minoritised women who are sexual violence survivors may seek criminal justice responses to their experiences, and therefore sets out detailed recommendations as to how those services must better respond to their needs and interests (Thiara and Roy, 2020).

Therefore, recognising that racism, as well as class, gender, age and immigration status, are key factors in how the criminal justice system responds to sexual violence, need not inexorably lead to disengaging with that problematic system. Multiple approaches are required: supporting victim-survivors who engage with the current criminal justice system; reforming that system to reduce its harmful impacts; and developing support and redress approaches beyond the criminal justice system (Thiara and Roy, 2020).

Justifying criminalisation

While holding on to the considerable power of some of the anti-criminalisation arguments, we set out here some possible justifications for turning to the criminal law, consistent with a multi-faceted approach to criminalisation.

Recognition and expressive justice

In defending feminist legal strategies, Mackinnon (2017, 330) argues that law 'can be a way to fight for change'. She continues that law can represent that people stand behind you, hear you and support you. Law can be a form of recognition, it can also mean hope: 'what happened to you might not happen to someone else, or to you, again'. In this way, law is not so much about incarceration ('that does so little right and so much wrong') or compensation 'however deserved as no amount fully compensates' (MacKinnon, 2017, 331). Its meaning is far broader; and lies in the possibility of law's capacity 'to restore some of the humanity their victimisation took away' (MacKinnon, 2017, 331).

This capacity and potential of the law to bring recognition comes through its constitutive power: its 'recognition of harm is of crucial importance in the struggle to ensure that women's voices are heard and understood' (Conaghan, 1996, 431). This is echoed by Crocker (2008, 110) who suggests that when we are considering the 'success' of laws, particularly measures to tackle violence against women, 'we need to shift our attention to how law makes meaning as an important measure of its transformative potential'. In particular, she argues that if we 'understand law to be constitutive of social processes, then the meaning it makes is as important as the punishment it supports' (Crocker, 2008, 110).

In this way, constructing cyberflashing as a criminal wrong may mean that for victim-survivors their experiences are recognised as harmful and wrong. Recognition, in this sense, conveys the understanding that they have been harmed and encompasses the significance of the experience being acknowledged. Recognition also entails an expectation or entitlement to consideration, to redress; it is a form of acknowledgement, conveying support. In essence, therefore, criminalisation of behaviour such as cyberflashing, whether or not a victim engages with the criminal justice system, can send a message to a victim-survivor: your harmful experience is acknowledged and understood; you are not alone; it is not your fault; you do not have to put up with it; it is not trivial; and something can be done about it. For some victim-survivors of sexual violence, such recognition can constitute a form of justice (McGlynn and Westmarland, 2019).

Law, therefore, has a powerful role in shaping how we understand behaviours and what they denote to victim-survivors. Intertwined with this constitutive power is law's authority to express that new meaning to society more broadly, as Citron explains: law 'shapes attitudes, beliefs, and behaviour through its messages and lessons' (Citron, 2019, 1945). Citron argues that law can also shift attitudes, noting that where 'public sentiment about specific behaviour is unclear, law provides expressive clarity, channelling shifts in beliefs, attitudes and behaviours' (Citron, 2019, 1946). In challenging wrongful behaviour in this way, the ambition is for law to effect of a 'wave of condemnation' (Kahan, 2000, 613) such that the actions under scrutiny become unconsciously avoided. In this way, it is the expressive role of law that is more significant than its coercive power. It is individual citizens who, in practice, enact and enforce the law by obeying it in daily life. Without this active compliance, especially in the fast-moving technological context of cyberflashing, the law would have little impact.

The expressive role of the criminal law, therefore, has two particular aspects. It addresses a form of hermeneutical injustice faced by victim-survivors whose experiences are not recognised (Fricker, 2007; Giladi, 2018); where victim–survivors struggle to be understood in a society where cyberflashing is trivialised and minimised, and therefore struggle to understand, narrate and name what has happened to them. Further, when seeking cultural change, harnessing the expressive power of law plays a role in communicating society's commitments and beliefs, and therefore shaping people's behaviour. Indeed, it is the potential deterrent and therefore educative aspect of law's role, rather than its punitive aspect per se, which can encourage cultural change (McGlynn and Rackley, 2017).

The 'under-criminalisation' of women's harms

The 'success' of law, therefore, may be felt in how it shapes our recognition and understanding of what is harmful, what conduct is wrongful, in how we understand and prevent specific behaviours, and in how we understand justice. Justifying the criminal law in this way may also help to refute some of the critiques of 'over-criminalisation', namely that countries such as the US and UK have overseen a vast mobilisation of the criminal law to regulate relatively harmless conduct (Husak, 2008). Franks, for example, has injected a welcome dose of gendered analysis into this debate, pointing out that while there may be an over-criminalisation of some activities, society has tended to under-criminalise and under-police harms primarily experienced by women (Franks, 2017, 1305). In the specific context of non-consensual pornography, therefore, she argues that as men's abuse of women is generally *under*, not over-criminalised, and in view of the seriousness of the privacy violations of these actions, the benefits of criminalisation outweigh the costs (Franks, 2017, 1308).

Further, the charge of over-criminalisation needs to take account of the fact that while there may well be some unjustified criminal laws, there are also many examples of harms predominantly experienced by women currently excluded from the criminal law. Moreover, even where there are existing laws covering specific activities, they often fail to be interpreted to include women's experiences. For example, many forms of harassment are criminalised, commonly those associated with the public sphere, but less so the more personal and targeted experiences of harassment such as cyberflashing. Therefore, while the criminal law already addresses *some* forms of harassment, the question becomes whether the current myopic coverage, excluding most experiences of cyberflashing, should continue; or whether criminalisation might represent the law (finally) 'catching up' with some women's experiences.

Harm to others and social utility

In this light, we also need to directly address whether the harms of cyberflashing meet the threshold commonly set out for coercive state power, namely that the criminal law should only be used where necessary to 'prevent harm to others' (John Stuart Mill, 1859, in Robson, 1977, 22). Harm, in this context, is commonly understood as a 'setback to interests', described as involving a 'diminution of one's opportunities to enjoy or pursue a good life' (Simester et al, 2013, 646). Von Hirsch and Jareborg (1991) suggest in more detail that there are four general interests which might be adversely affected: physical integrity, material support, freedom from humiliation or degrading treatment, and privacy and autonomy. Drawing on the analysis in previous chapters, it is apparent that cyberflashing can produce significant harms, being a clear example of harms to privacy, autonomy and constituting humiliation and degrading treatment. While we noted that not every person experiences cyberflashing in these ways, criminalisation can follow where not every instance of conduct is itself demonstrably harmful, such as with vehicle speeding. It is the risks of speeding that are considerable, justifying criminal sanctions, in the same way that the risks of cyberflashing are great.

Further, there is little social utility in speeding which introduces us to the need to also balance the different rights, risks and harms, with the overall social value of behaviours. As Simester et al set out: a 'responsible legislator should, therefore, consider the gravity and likelihood of the wrongful harm and weigh that against the social value of the conduct to be prohibited and the degree of intrusion upon citizen's lives that criminalisation would involve' (2013, 649). When we undertake this balancing exercise in relation to cyberflashing, while we can identify the wrong in the non-consensual conduct, and the risk of significant harms, it is possible that some individuals will gain, including through sexual arousal or developing sexual relationships. Nonetheless, what remains important is that the acts to be criminalised are not the sharing of penis images per se – which might be said to be overly restrictive bearing in mind any social utility – but the *non-consensual* distribution of images. Therefore, the benefits of sexual pleasure, for example, can still be achieved through securing consent for sharing images, meaning that any restriction on non-consensual activity is not disproportionate.

Beyond punitive punishment

In advancing arguments in favour of criminalisation, not only is it important to challenge existing practices which may have ignored the harms experienced by particular groups, but we should also seek to shift discourse and policy away from assuming that criminalisation leads automatically to penalism and punitive sanctions. Norrie writes of the problem of the assumed 'penal equation' which requires that 'crime plus responsibility equals punishment' (2005, 75). This is only one conception, even if dominant, of the role and outcome of criminalisation, but it is not inevitable (Lacey and Pickard, 2015). That is, crime plus responsibility need not lead inexorably towards punishment, but can be about recognition, prevention and a variety of alternative consequences (McGlynn and Westmarland, 2019). This echoes Gotell (2015, 67) who talks of the need to combine a critical analysis of criminal law with 'renewed attention to diverse extra-legal strategies that would re-politicise the problem of sexual assault and offer alternative responses'. This is because 'feminists have pursued law reform strategies to gain recognition of the harms caused by sexual assault, not to punish and incarcerate perpetrators' (Gotell, 2015, 69).

In specific terms, this would mean criminalising cyberflashing – signalling the wrongdoing, harm and need for redress – but without that redress inevitably being carceral, punitive punishment. The aim, therefore, is to develop policy that does not *prioritise* or *prefer* criminal sanctioning, or treat criminal law as the *best* way forward, but to have it as one of many options, albeit one that can provide a foundation for condemning conduct. This approach can chime with those who critique criminalisation. While Gruber (2020, 17) argues that criminal law should be a 'last, not first, resort' for feminists, we would argue that it can be one amongst many equally important strategies, but specifically that the *punitive enforcement* of criminal law should be the last resort. As Franks (2017, 130 2) suggests: 'Criminalisation is not synonymous with incarceration, and incarceration is not synonymous with mandatory minimums or lengthy sentences.'

Criminalisation, therefore, does not preclude alternatives to carceral punishment (Terweil, 2020). Indeed, we would argue that recognising the justice interests of victim-survivors of sexual violence requires us to engage with a whole range of 'consequences' for perpetrating harm, particularly non-punitive responses (Herman, 2005; Daly, 2014; Holder, 2015; McGlynn and Westmarland, 2019). Kim identifies a strengthening anti-gender violence and anti-criminalisation coalition among a growing 'cross-racial group of anti-violence advocates, legal scholars and feminist and racial justice advocates' (Kim, 2018,

225). This movement mobilises around prison abolition and alternative visions for violence prevention and intervention, often focussing on transformative and restorative justice principles (Kim, 2018, 225).

This reflects similar movements in the UK where the justice interests of sexual violence survivors are increasingly recognised as complex, nuanced, variable and going beyond the criminal justice system: characterised in some contexts by the notion of 'kaleidoscopic justice' (McGlynn and Westmarland, 2019). This approach builds on policies and practices around transformative justice (Smith, 2010; Dixon and Lakshmi Piepzna-Samarasinha, 2020) and restorative justice (McGlynn et al, 2012; Zinsstag and Keenan, 2017) as responses to sexual violence. Such approaches are also of interest to survivors of street harassment (Fileborn and Vera-Gray, 2017), as well as online abuse, with a recent study on image-based sexual abuse finding that while some survivors sought a police response, others favoured more restorative approaches (McGlynn et al, 2019). A more nuanced approach to criminalisation may help us to envisage a variety of responses to behaviours such as cyberflashing, including punishment as a last resort, but also interventions prioritising non-punitive and non-carceral rehabilitation, prevention and education (Terweil, 2020).

Conclusions

While Carol Smart warned against the siren call of law, she also reflected that de-centring law did not mean ignoring or abandoning it as a site of struggle (Smart, 2012, 162). Indeed, Smart acknowledges that law has a 'positive capacity' to 'offer recognition and affirmation' (quoted in Auchmuty and Van Marle, 2012, 66). Further, even if we choose to disengage, law's power is not diminished. Law will continue to shape, influence and determine much of our lives, whatever strategy we adopt.

Therefore, and in relation to cyberflashing specific-ally, without change, the law will continue to neglect and marginalise the harms experienced by women, failing to recognise them or provide redress. Engaging with the law, therefore, is a complex equation: seeking to harness its transformative power, while resisting its capacity to distract and reinforce disadvantage. Our aim in this book is to engage with the criminal law as part of a holistic strategy to generate change, with the hope of fostering greater equality, liberty and freedom.

FOUR

Cyberflashing and the Limits of English Criminal Law

If this offence isn't covered by existing laws, then it should be legislated for as it's not acceptable.

(Hannah, quoted in Gallagher, 2019a)

The criminal law in England and Wales is currently failing victim-survivors of cyberflashing. Despite its prevalence and potentially harmful impacts, cyberflashing is not clearly a criminal act, leaving victims and criminal justice personnel navigating a labyrinth of possible offences. This is not to suggest that cyberflashing cannot be prosecuted: it could be. However, the law is not clear, the hurdles are many and therefore prosecutions are unlikely.

Before making the case for broader law reform in the chapters that follow, we examine here the current English criminal law as it might be applied to cyberflashing. We identify the many challenges facing any prosecution, including requirements to prove motives that are not always present or dominant in cyberflashing cases; demonstrating that penis images are applicable to provisions centring on morality-based concepts such as indecency, obscenity and offensiveness; and navigating laws which protect people in physical, public spaces, rather than in online environments. In essence, the law has ultimately failed to keep pace with the emergent ways in which sexual violence is being perpetrated through new and evolving technological mediums.

Cyberflashing as a sexual offence?

As cyberflashing constitutes a sexual intrusion, and parallels other forms of criminalised sexual violence, we first examine the applicability of existing sexual offences. As there is a criminal law against 'flashing' – section 66 of the Sexual Offences Act 2003 – it might be assumed this covers cyberflashing. Given the similarities between the two forms of abuse, there appears to be no reason why this should not be the case. However, it is unlikely that the 'sexual exposure' offence applies to cyberflashing.

This offence was first introduced in the 2003 Act, replacing the previous nineteenth-century provisions which addressed men exposing their penis. The prosecution have to prove that the offender 'intentionally exposes his genitals', meaning that an image of someone else's penis will not suffice, and that 'he intends that someone will see them and be caused alarm or distress'. This specific motive requirement was introduced to avoid prosecution of naturists who may expose themselves without any harmful intent. However, this motive requirement also excludes some perpetrators, most obviously where the motivation is sexual gratification. The words 'alarm or distress' have been interpreted as requiring 'real emotional disturbance or upset' (Rook and Ward, 2016, para 15.196).

The key question, for our purposes, is whether online exposure comes within this provision. While the original focus was physical acts of exposure, there is nothing which specific-ally precludes its application to cyberflashing. It is possible to prosecute online exposure in real time, such as in *R v Alderton* (2014)[1] where the offender exposed himself via Facetime. However, a recent Law Commission review commented that the offence relates to 'an act in real-time rather than the distri-bution and possession of images and recordings' and therefore is likely to only apply to 'live-streamed' online exposure, though

---

[1]   *R v Alderton* [2014] EWCA Crim 2204.

it noted that this has not been tested in law (2018, 135). There is no reason in principle why this offence could not apply, though it seems unlikely that prosecutions will be brought.

There are further offences within the 2003 Act that apply specifically to children which provide some additional protections, and do apply to live online activities (CPS, 2020). The offences of 'causing a child to watch a sexual act' (section 12) and 'sexual communication' with a child (section 15A) were introduced to target sexual grooming. Unfortunately, cyberflashing does not fit these well. The observation in section 12 must be of 'sexual activity' and it is not clear whether this might be limited to an erect penis or video. While the scope of section 15A is broader, with 'sexual communication' likely to cover all penis images, it is – like section 12 – limited to victim-survivors under the age of 16.

The differing aims and purposes of these provisions is reflected in the differing motive requirements, with the sexual exposure offence requiring a motive to cause distress, and proof of sexual gratification for the children's offences. Nonetheless, the children's provisions may provide some redress, even if only for some forms of cyberflashing.

Cyberflashing as indecent and a public outrage?

Another option is the archaic common law offence of 'outraging public decency'. This offence has been applied to a wide range of public nuisances, including sexual activity in public and 'upskirting', and could conceivably apply to cyberflashing (Law Commission, 2018, 132–136). However, this is not as straightforward as it might be hoped.

First, it is not clear exactly what constitutes an outrage against public decency. The conduct must be 'lewd, obscene or disgusting' (*R v May* [1989], 159)[2] and go beyond 'offending

---

[2]   *R v May* (1989) 91 Cr App R 157.

the susceptibilities of, or even shocking, reasonable people' (*Knuller v DPP* (1973), para 495C).[3] Whether or not an act may outrage depends on the circumstances, including the location, time, duration, consent or non-consent, and who was present (Rook and Ward, 2016, para 15.44). The parameters of this offence, therefore, are not clear and what falls within its scope is going to vary considerably over time and across communities. Nonetheless, it is possible, perhaps likely, that sending an unsolicited penis image would constitute 'lewd, obscene or disgusting' behaviour, as the offence has previously been used for 'upskirting', other forms of public exposure, and sexual activities in public (Law Commission, 2015, para 2.37).

However, the conduct must also have outraged the 'public', interpreted as requiring more than one person being present and able to see the act (*R v May* (1989))[4] which may prove difficult in cyberflashing cases where only one person receives the image. The electronic nature of the communication may also pose difficulties, with the Law Commission noting there are no known cases of this offence being carried out online (2018, para 6.111).

Ironically, it may be easier to use this offence to prosecute the victim of cyberflashing who shows the image to another, perhaps in shock and seeking support (Law Commission, 2015, para 2.47; McGlynn, 2017). Therefore, while cyberflashing might technically fall within this offence, it seems the difficulties of establishing the act outraged the 'public' mean it is not going to prove useful.

Similarly, legislation proscribing the display of 'indecent' materials, which might at first glance be considered a possibility, only extends to matters visible from any 'public place' (section 1, Indecent Displays (Control) Act 1981). This legislation, designed to limit shop displays of sexually explicit magazines,

---

[3] *Knuller v DPP* [1973] AC 435.
[4] *R v May* [1989] 91 Cr App R 157.

is unlikely therefore to challenge online distribution of penis images and, even if it applied in some circumstances, it will not cover cyberflashing occurring in the wide range of private, online settings.

Beyond the hurdles of demonstrating that cyberflashing took place in, and offended, the 'public', these offences are not especially suitable for addressing cyberflashing, because they do not recognise its sexual nature or impacts. Cyberflashing is not merely a 'nuisance' or offensive to the public: it is a sexual intrusion which violates sexual autonomy, and can cause significant harm to individuals.

Cyberflashing as harassment?

Perhaps laws focussing on harassment may provide a better avenue for redress, tying more closely to victim–survivors' experiences. While there is no general criminal law covering sexual harassment, where there is repeated harassment, the Protection from Harassment Act 1997 may provide a remedy. Enacted partly in response to women's experiences of stalking and harassment, the Act makes it an offence to harass someone as part of a 'course of conduct' (section 2), or to put them in fear of violence by such a course of conduct. Harassment is interpreted as 'causing alarm or distress' (section 7) and includes repeated attempts to impose unwanted communications on an individual, in a manner that could be expected to cause distress or fear in any reasonable person – such as the repeated sending of unsolicited penis images.

Nonetheless, the conduct must be sufficiently harmful that it crosses 'the boundary between conduct which is unattractive, even unreasonable, and conduct which is oppressive and unacceptable' (*Majrowski v Guy's and Thomas' NHS Trust* [2007], para 30).[5] The commonplace trivialisation of cyberflashing risks

---

[5]   *Majrowski v Guy's and Thomas' NHS Trust* [2007] 1 AC 224.

that it is not perceived as crossing this threshold into criminality. It must also be shown that the offender knew or ought to have known that the conduct amounts to harassment. A conviction, therefore, will only follow if a 'reasonable person' would consider two or more instances of cyberflashing as constituting a *criminal* level of 'harassment'; a potentially difficult threshold in light of the 'reasonable person' historically often failing to understand women's experiences (West, 1987; Graycar and Morgan, 2002; Conaghan, 2013).

It is possible that the legislation might apply where cyberflashing forms part of a broader pattern of harassing behaviour. The Crown Prosecution Service (CPS) recognises stalking and harassment can be perpetrated online (2018, para 43), and that cyberstalking can be combined with other forms of harassment such as 'threatening or obscene emails or text messages'. Nevertheless, while cyberflashing might form part of a pattern of harassment, a one-time distribution will not be covered, nor is it clear that even repeated acts of cyberflashing will have sufficient weight to lead to a prosecution.

While the Protection from Harassment Act focuses on harassment targeting specific individuals, harassment is also an important element of a range of public order offences. The Public Order Act 1986 provides two potential avenues for redress, namely section 4A covering 'intentional harassment, alarm or distress', or section 5 covering 'harassment, alarm or distress'. However, as the Law Commission noted, applying the public order offences to online communications 'presents some real challenges' (2020, para 3.67).

Specifically, there are several thresholds in section 4A which make prosecution unlikely. First, the act must be found to constitute a threatening, abusive or insulting 'visible representation'. While victim-survivors' accounts in earlier chapters demonstrate cyberflashing can be experienced as threatening and abusive, whether it is so understood by criminal justice personnel is less obvious. An instructive example comes from a Scottish cases involving a 'pick-up artist' (Roach, 2020) who targeted women, seeking to engage them in conversation in public streets, blocking their movements, sometimes touching or attempting to kiss them, giving 'compliments' and seeking their personal details (*Ahmed v Her Majesty's Advocate* (2020)).[6]

Ahmed was charged with 'threatening or abusive behaviour', similar to the English public order offences, but his convictions were quashed on appeal as 'there was nothing in the appellant's behaviour … which was overtly threatening or which could reasonably be construed as threatening' (para 51). The behaviour was interpreted by the (male) judges as a 'polite conversational request or compliment' which cannot be construed as threatening 'merely because it is uninvited or unwelcome' (para 51). This judgment displays a concerning lack of understanding of the nature of public harassment experienced by many women (Vera-Gray, 2016; 2017a). That behaviour is not *overtly* threatening does not mean it is not experienced as such; more concerning still is the assumption that the behaviour could not 'reasonably' be interpreted as threatening. There is clearly a gulf between what is understood by the senior judiciary as 'reasonable' and the common experiences of women. While there are differences between the English and Scottish offences, each are underpinned by understandings of what might constitute threatening or abusive behaviour and intentions. This example indicates a worryingly low level of understanding among some groups of women's everyday experiences of public harassment, which includes cyberflashing.

Even if this element of the offence was satisfied, a particular motive – intention to cause harassment, alarm or distress – must also be demonstrated. We know from non-consensual distribution of intimate image cases that this threshold is challenging and acts as a disincentive to police and prosecutors (McGlynn et al, 2019). This may be even more likely in cyberflashing cases where often there are only image/s distributed, with

---

[6]   *Ahmed v Her Majesty's Advocate* [2020] HJAC 37.

no additional text or actions from which to draw an inference. Further, even where the behaviour is experienced as threatening and abusive, this may not be the sender's intention. Finally, this offence requires proof of a particular result, namely that the victim was in fact harmed. While this may be possible in many cases, it is a further invasion of victim–survivors' privacy and an unnecessary burden. Moreover, the victim who is understandably incensed by this conduct, but has not suffered demonstrable harm, will have no redress under this legislation.

An alternative might be prosecution under section 5, which focuses on the perpetrator's behaviour. This, however, requires the defendant 'displays any writing, sign or other visible representation which is threatening or abusive', or 'uses threatening or abusive words or behaviour', and that the conduct take place 'within the hearing or sight of a person likely to be caused harassment, alarm or distress'. The defendant must also intend, or be aware, their words or behaviour are threatening or abusive. Accordingly, it is not obvious this offence would cover cyberflashing. While cyberflashing via Bluetooth might be 'within the hearing or sight' of someone likely to be caused harassment, alarm or distress, such an interpretation would require a more innovative approach to prosecutions, and recognition that the conduct itself is 'threatening or abusive'.

Therefore, the public order offences, if applicable, will only cover some forms of cyberflashing, and even then, proving the images fall within the provisions will be challenging. And, as 'public order' offences, they do not apply to conduct occurring in private, further limiting their scope. In many ways, this is not surprising because these offences were simply not 'designed to assist victims of sexual harassment' (Mackay and Earnshaw, 1995, 340).

Cyberflashing as a problematic communication?

This leads us to one final option and to what are commonly known as the communications offences. Cyberflashing perhaps should be covered by the offence of distributing sexual images without consent, sometimes referred to as 'revenge porn', though better understood as image-based sexual abuse (McGlynn and Rackley, 2017). However, that offence was drafted to require the non-consent of the person *in the image*, not the recipient, mirroring similar legislation in other jurisdictions.

We are, therefore, left with section 1 of the Malicious Communications Act 1988 (MCA) and section 127 of the Communications Act 2003. First introduced in the 1980s to criminalise 'poison pen' letters and other abusive and threatening communications (Law Commission, 2018, para 4.10) they have been applied to a wide range of online communications. However, cyberflashing will only come within these offences if it can be shown that one of the purposes of sending the penis image was to cause distress or anxiety to the recipient and that the message was indecent or grossly offensive.

Specifically, section 1 of the MCA requires the perpetrator to have sent an indecent or grossly offensive message, including electronic communications, to a specific person/s, with the intention of causing distress or anxiety. There is no definition of 'grossly offensive', it being a malleable concept determined by the jury or magistrates engaging a 'reasonable person' test (Law Commission, 2018, para 5.46). CPS guidelines (2018) state there should only be a prosecution for gross offensiveness when the communication amounts to more than something 'offensive, shocking or disturbing'. It is uncertain whether a penis image meets this threshold. Guidance emerges from a case where a man photoshopped penises onto a picture of a policeman and uploaded it to Facebook (*Daily Mail*, 2014; Law Commission, 2018, para 5.75). Though the image was of a police officer on duty, it is unclear why this was 'grossly offensive', but perhaps is indicative of penis images coming within this legislation.

The law is similarly vague about what constitutes 'indecency' which sometimes includes nudity, particularly regarding child sexual abuse images, but less clearly adult nudity (Law Commission, 2018, para 6.85). It might be that an erect penis image is more likely to satisfy this threshold. However, it remains unclear, as terms such as 'indecency' and 'obscenity' are often interpreted by those who dominate decision-making and public narratives, marginalising perspectives from women, particularly those from black and minoritised communities (Crenshaw, 1991; Vera-Gray and McGlynn, 2020).

If the content satisfies the indecency or grossly offensive threshold, it must also be proven that the purpose, or 'one of the purposes' in sending the message, is to 'cause distress or anxiety' to the recipient. The Law Commission noted the aim is to ensure a defendant cannot avoid a charge by claiming a different, perhaps legitimate, purpose (2018, para 4.41). For example, in *Connolly v DPP* (2007),[7] which involved sending photos of aborted foetuses to pharmacies selling emergency contraception, the accused was convicted despite her stated purpose being 'education', because it was inferred another purpose was to cause distress.

Section 127 provides that an offence is committed where a person sends a message or other matter that is 'grossly offensive or of an indecent, obscene or menacing character' by means of a 'public communications network'. The scope is similar to the MCA, though with the addition of 'menacing', which may be particularly pertinent for cyberflashing cases. CPS guidance emphasises the material must be 'more than ... offensive, shocking or disturbing' (2018), again making it unclear whether a penis image will satisfy the required threshold.

If the threshold is met, it must be proven both that the perpetrator intended to send the message and that they had an intention to insult those to whom the message relates, or were aware of the risk of doing so (Law Commission, 2018, para 4.97). Regarding 'menacing', there must be proof of awareness

---

[7] *Connolly v DPP* [2007] EWHC 237 (Admin).

or recognition of a risk that sending the message may create fear or apprehension in any reasonable member of the public who reads or sees it. Actual harm in a victim need not be proven. This is a lower threshold than for the MCA (Law Commission, 2018, para 4.93) but still requires demonstration that the perpetrator had an aim in mind other than sexual gratification or amusement. Even if these thresholds are met, the peculiarity of these provisions means that only images sent via a 'public communications network' are covered. Private or restricted networks, such as those used in some workplaces, will not be covered, nor will Bluetooth or AirDrop, thus underlining that these forms of legislation are no longer suitable for regulating everyday life.

As well as the technological and other limitations of the communications offences, characterising cyberflashing as a 'problematic communication' fails to recognise its nature and harms. Overall, therefore, securing a prosecution using these offences is challenging. Nevertheless, the Malicious Communications Act does provide one option for redress, and is the offence under which police record cyberflashing reports, though recent data found only one arrest out of 66 recent reports (Bowden, 2020; Gallagher, 2020).

Conclusions

English criminal law is failing victim-survivors of cyberflashing as there are no clear means by which to prosecute this practice. While there are several offences which could be utilised, each are beset by constraints and limitations. The offences are often focussed on the impact on the public, rather than on the harms experienced by targeted individuals. This not only fails to recognise who are the true victims, but also restricts the application of the offences by requiring more than one person to experience the conduct.

Another constraint is these offences mostly require proof of specific perpetrator motivations, particularly causing distress or alarm. Cyberflashing, however, is perpetrated for a variety of reasons, including causing distress and alarm, but also for sexual gratification, for so-called amusement, and for power and control. Thus, the motive requirements limit the cyberflashing contexts captured within these provisions.

Even if these thresholds are met, what remains largely untested is whether penis images would fall within these provisions. Is a penis image indecent, obscene, or such that someone is understandably outraged? It could be argued that a penis image, like any nudity, is not per se offensive or indecent, though an erect penis image might satisfy these criteria. But it would be unsound to have an offence criminalising an unsolicited image of an erect, but not flaccid, penis. Finally, while the sexual exposure offence closely matches cyberflashing conduct, it is widely presumed this offence does not apply to cyberflashing, with no apparent appetite for testing this assumption.

There are two further overarching explanations as to why the criminal law is failing victim-survivors. The first is the inability of current provisions to encompass evolving technology. For example, the 'public' focus relates to impacts on the public as individuals and also that the acts take place in conventional public places. Outraging public decency and public order offences, for example, are focussed on curbing nuisance and disorder in outdoor, physical spaces. Online crimes of all sorts, including cyberflashing, are challenging this way of understanding what constitutes a public space, but this is yet to have a significant impact on the criminal law.

The second more conceptual explanation is, simply, that the law fails to recognise, understand and tackle women's experiences. Cyberflashing, like many harms experienced predominantly by women, falls between the gaps and categories of English criminal law. As with other forms of harassment and abuse that have thrived with developing technology, such as image-based sexual abuse, these experiences defy existing categories. Feminist lawyers have long argued that the law fails to understand and reflect women's experiences of harm (Dahl,

1987; Graycar and Morgan, 2002; Munro, 2007; Conaghan, 2013). While Liz Kelly rightly recognises there are 'no clearly defined and discrete analytic categories' into which 'men's behaviour can be placed' (1988, 7), the challenge is that to provide some redress via the criminal law, we must work to organise the law such that it reflects, supports and challenges the harms experienced by women.

Given its harms, cyberflashing requires a coherent legal response that adequately expresses societal condemnation, and meets demands for justice, redress and change. The current fragmented, ad hoc and reactive approach is inadequate. A first step towards remedying this is to introduce a specific law criminalising cyberflashing, paralleling steps taken by several other countries. The next chapter considers these developments, before proceeding to make the case for a bespoke cyberflashing offence in England and Wales.

FIVE

Cyberflashing Laws: Comparative Perspectives

> It is the same as physical exposure and it should be treated as such.
>
> (Gail, quoted in Gallagher, 2019a)

While English criminal law struggles to bring cyberflashing within existing offences, the situation is different in many other countries. Scotland, for example, has longstanding sexual offences legislation which is sufficiently broad that it extends to new modes of perpetration like cyberflashing. Other countries, such as Singapore, have recently updated their law, ensuring that emergent forms of sexual offending, including cyberflashing, are criminalised. And in the last few years, several US states have introduced specific criminal offences to directly target cyberflashing. This chapter examines these various provisions to identify the lessons to be learnt, particularly considering their conceptual foundations, the scope of the offences, as well as any motive or intention requirements. This analysis lays the foundation for our recommendations regarding criminal law reform outlined in the following chapter.

Scotland: Coercing a person to look at a sexual image

When revising its sexual offence laws over ten years ago, Scotland aimed to introduce a criminal code which better reflected the nature, breadth and harms of sexual offending (Scottish Law Commission, 2006; 2007). While there will always be gaps and new challenges to be met, this general approach has reaped benefits. Before cyberflashing was even imagined, these new sexual offence laws included provisions sufficiently broad to encompass these emerging ways of perpetrating harm.

Specifically, the Sexual Offences (Scotland) Act 2009 includes the offence of 'coercing a person into looking at a sexual image' (section 6).[1] This was introduced following a Scottish Law Commission consultation that considered the English sexual offence of 'causing a person to engage in sexual activity' (section 4, Sexual Offences Act 2003). Both jurisdictions recognised sexual offending includes non-contact activities, characterised by the Scottish Law Commission as 'coercive'. However, while English law only provides for the offence of causing another to *engage in* sexual activity, the Scottish Law Commission recognised that coercive behaviour is more complex and can include the use of images and written materials.

Accordingly, the Scottish Law Commission recommended an offence of making a sexual communication without consent

---

[1] Section 6, Sexual Offences (Scotland) Act 2009: Coercing a person into looking at a sexual image
  (1) If a person ('A') intentionally and for a purpose mentioned in subsection (2) causes another person ('B') –
    (a) without B consenting, and
    (b) without any reasonable belief that B consents, to look at a sexual image, then A commits an offence, to be known as the offence of coercing a person into looking at a sexual image.
  (2) The purposes are –
    (a) obtaining sexual gratification,
    (b) humiliating, distressing or alarming B.
  (3) For the purposes of subsection (1), a sexual image is an image (produced by whatever means and whether or not a moving image) of –
    (a) A engaging in a sexual activity or of a third person or imaginary person so engaging,
    (b) A's genitals or the genitals of a third person or imaginary person.

(2007, para 3.62). It noted that England's offences of engaging in sexual activity in the presence of a child and causing a child to watch sexual activity (sections 11 and 12, Sexual Offences Act 2003) only applied to children and sexual gratification was a required motive (Scottish Law Commission, 2007, para 3.58). The Scottish Law Commission rejected both limitations as being too constraining, noting that 'just as being forced to participate in sexual activity is an invasion of a person's sexual autonomy, so is being forced to watch such activity' (2007, para 3.55).

Unfortunately, the resulting provision was more limited than that proposed by the Law Commission. Section 6 of the Sexual Offences (Scotland) Act 2009 created the offence of 'coercing a person into looking at a sexual image' for the purposes of sexual gratification or humiliating, distressing or alarming the victim. This requires proof of intentionally 'causing' another to look at a sexual image without their consent, rather than the more straightforward distribution or making of the communication. Sections 23 and 33 of the Act provide for similar offences in relation to children and young people.

Unfortunately, this leaves some gaps. For example, if the victim did not view the image, the offence is not made out. Specific motives must also be proven, though this at least includes intention to humiliate, alarm and distress, as well as sexual gratification. The guidance states these motive requirements are necessary to exclude bona fide activities such as a biology school teacher using genital images. It is right that this should not constitute a criminal offence, although such consensual activities would likely be excluded.

Other elements of the offence are sufficiently broad to encompass a range of sexual harms, including cyberflashing. For example, 'sexual image' is widely defined, covering images of the perpetrator's or another's genitals, without the requirement to prove the image is of the offender's penis. In addition, other 'sexual activity' of the offender, another or an 'imaginary person' is also included. In effect, the offence extends beyond the non-consensual distribution of penis images to general material depicting sexual activity: encompassing, in essence, coercing someone to view pornography. Finally, it covers fake and photoshopped images, particularly prescient given the fast-developing technology making 'deepfake' pornographic videos increasingly common (Chesney and Citron, 2019; Burgess, 2020).

While this offence enables cyberflashing prosecutions, there is unfortunately little information on its deployment. Freedom of Information data reveals that, since the law was introduced, there have been 3,115 reports of adults coercing other adults into looking at sexual images, and 1,962 reports of children being victims (Gallagher, 2019h). Because of the breadth of the offence, we do not know how these figures relate to cyberflashing. However, they do include some cyberflashing prosecutions and convictions for other sexual offences following reports of cyberflashing (Gallagher, 2019h).

Accordingly, there are important lessons to be learnt from Scots law. First, being framed as a sexual offence means the nature and harms of the conduct is appropriately acknowledged and, in applying to adults and children, everyone's rights to sexual autonomy are recognised. Second, this provision was originally introduced due to concerns about coercive sexual activity more generally, not cyberflashing, emphasising the importance of 'future-proofing' the law by not unduly limiting its scope. Third, it includes altered images and there is no restrictive requirement to prove an image is of an offender's penis. The introduction of this measure has proved prescient: the generic focus on activity led to the drafting of a broad provision which is able to be used in rapidly changing circumstances, such as the technical revolution enabling cyberflashing.

Ireland: Intentionally engaging in 'offensive conduct of a sexual nature'

Ireland provides another example of a sexual offence sufficiently broadly crafted that it may provide redress in some cases of cyberflashing. Section 45(3) of the Criminal Law (Sexual Offences) Act 2017 provides that an offence is committed where a person 'intentionally engages in offensive conduct of a sexual nature', defined as 'any behaviour of a sexual nature which, having regard to all the circumstances, is likely to cause fear, distress or alarm to any person who is, or might reasonably be expected to be, aware of any such behaviour' (section 45(6)). During legislative debates, the then Minister for Justice and Equality stated this provision sets an 'objective test of what might reasonably be considered offensive, having regard to all the circumstances' – meaning that the provision does not cover offensive material per se, but that it will only cover material deemed offensive by 'many' (Fitzgerald, 2016).

It is unclear where this leaves cyberflashing. As previously discussed, a penis image is not necessarily sexual per se, though it may well be classed as such, particularly an erect penis. Interestingly, the English Law Commission recently commented that, as a matter of 'common sense', cyberflashing is conduct of a 'sexual nature' (2020, para 6.124). Cyberflashing *can* induce fear, distress or alarm, though there may be debate around whether such impacts are 'likely', whether an offender is expected to be aware of such effects, and whether 'many' people would find this conduct 'offensive'.

This measure is included alongside provisions on sexual exposure and other sexual acts in public and was introduced to replace previous indecency offences (O'Malley, 2017). Interestingly, while the Scottish provision reflects an understanding of the breadth and nature of coercive sexual behaviours, the Irish provision is more related to morality-based concerns over public decency. While the effect of the measure may be similar to the Scottish provisions, the conduct is labelled as 'offensive' which speaks more to being affronted, rather than rights to sexual autonomy being breached. This conceptual difference likely hinders public awareness regarding the potential of this measure to target cyberflashing, with few victims or criminal justice personnel being aware of its possibilities. This conceptualisation might also be limited in practice, particularly when considering what constitutes 'all the circumstances' and the 'likelihood' of fear, alarm or distress.

Irish law also has a general provision on physical exposure which, like its English equivalent, does not necessarily preclude cyberflashing, though the assumption is that it does (section 45(1) of the Criminal Law (Sexual Offences) Act 2017). In addition, there are offences protecting children from being exposed to visual sexual materials, including 'causing a child to watch sexual activity' in section 6 of the Criminal Law (Sexual Offences) Act 2017. This offence involves causing a child (person aged under 17) to 'look at an image of that person or another person engaging in sexual activity'. Like Scotland, this offence requires the child to view the image and it remains uncertain whether a penis image would constitute sexual 'activity'.

Irish law provides some means to prosecute cyberflashing, though these possibilities are not widely known, rendering the expressive value of the criminal law largely otiose. Nonetheless, there remains real potential here to provide a basis for reform which again demonstrates the value of broadly drafted provisions that can adapt to changing circumstances.

Singapore: New offence of sexual exposure

The alternative to a broad offence is one deliberately targeting cyberflashing, such as in Singapore where, since January 2020, cyberflashing has constituted a specific criminal offence. The law was introduced as part of an overhaul of Singapore's criminal code, following concern over the 'pervasive' nature of 'digital sexual violence' (Lih Yi, 2019; Vitis, 2020). In 2018, the Penal Code Review Committee (PCRC) recommended new laws covering voyeurism, distributing and threatening to distribute intimate images, and sexual exposure (Ministry of Law, 2018).

The existing law did cover some cases of exposure, including appearing in public nude, obscene songs and gestures insulting a woman's modesty, but it was argued these provisions did not fully capture the extent and range of offending, including sexual exposure in private settings, and the penalties were too low (PCRC, 2018, 86; Hussain, 2019). Also, the PCRC (2018, 86) noted the existing exposure offence was not listed as a 'sexual offence', and neither captured the sexual or malicious motives, nor the 'essence' of the wrongdoing. While cyberflashing was not included in the initial PCRC report, the Government subsequently revised its proposals to extend the sexual exposure offence to include cyberflashing after taking 'into account feedback from the law community' (Kwang, 2019). The new sexual offence is committed where a person intentionally distributes to another an image of their or another's genitals, intending that the victim see the image, and that the offender does so for the purpose of obtaining sexual gratification, or of causing the victim humiliation, distress or alarm (section 377BF Singapore Penal Code).[2]

The new law is relatively broad, which should facilitate prosecutions. It extends to genital images of the perpetrator or another, eschewing the largely insurmountable requirement of proof that the penis in the image belongs to the offender,

---

[2] Section 377BF, Singapore Penal Code:
  (1) Any person (A) shall be guilty of an offence who —
      (a) intentionally exposes A's genitals;
      (b) intends that another person (B) will see A's genitals; and
      (c) does so without B's consent for the purpose of obtaining sexual gratification or of causing B humiliation, distress or alarm.
  (2) Any person (A) shall be guilty of an offence who —
      (a) intentionally distributes to another person (B) an image of A's or any other person's genitals;
      (b) intends that B will see A's or the other person's genitals; and
      (c) does so without B's consent for the purpose of obtaining sexual gratification or of causing B humiliation, distress or alarm.

and recognising that the harm experienced is not dependent on the penis in the image belonging to a particular offender. As the offence involves non-consensual *distribution* rather than receipt, there is no requirement for the victim to receive or view the image. This is a welcome step compared, for example, to the Scottish provisions which require the victim to view the image. The focus on distribution may also make it easier to align this offence with other forms of image-based sexual abuse where distribution without consent is the key focus of the law.

However, other aspects of the law are more problematic. While its motive requirements include sexual gratification and intention to cause distress, this still excludes cyberflashing motivated by status-building, humour, or as a 'prank' (Livingstone, 2018). One simple way to extend the reach of the law would be to have included reckless intention, thereby including perpetrators who are aware that sending the unsolicited images may cause alarm or distress, even where this is not their direct intention. Notwithstanding these limitations, overall, this new offence is a welcome recognition of the nature of cyberflashing, characterising it as a sexual offence and covering a relatively broad range of cyberflashing contexts.

United States: From penis images to unsolicited pornography

Criminal laws across the US vary from state to state, with many, if not all, having prohibitions on persistent harassment, stalking and physical sexual exposure ('flashing'). As under English law, cyberflashing may come within some of these provisions, as well as other public order or related offences, but the overall picture is unclear and the thresholds for action preclude most instances. However, there are some states which have introduced specific measures to tackle cyberflashing, with many others considering action.

Texas: Unlawful electronic transmission of sexually explicit material

In 2019, Texas became the first US state to introduce a specific state law criminalising cyberflashing, following concern about the prevalence of this practice on dating and hook-up apps. Particularly, Bumble, a dating app oriented to making online dating safer and better for women, carried out a user survey and found one third of women had 'received unsolicited lewd photos from someone they hadn't yet met in person'; moreover, an 'overwhelming number of these women — 96 per cent— were unhappy to have been sent these images' (Bumble, nd).

The legislative sponsors stated that the current law 'addresses the physical act of indecent exposure, but is silent to the increasingly prevalent occurrence of individuals sending sexually explicit images to an individual without their consent' (Closson, 2019). Accordingly, a new criminal offence was added to the sexual offences chapter of the penal code, creating the offence of 'unlawful electronic transmission of sexually explicit visual material', with a maximum penalty of a $500 fine (section 21.19 Texas Penal Code).[3] The offence involves

---

[3] Section 1, Chapter 21, Texas Penal Code, is amended by adding Section 21.19 to read as follows: Sec. 21.19. Unlawful electronic transmission of sexually explicit visual material.

       (a) In this section, 'intimate parts', 'sexual conduct', and 'visual material' have the meanings assigned by Section 21.16.

       (b) A person commits an offense if the person knowingly transmits by electronic means visual material that:

  (1) depicts:

       (A) any person engaging in sexual conduct or with the person's intimate parts exposed; or

       (B) covered genitals of a male person that are in a discernibly turgid state; and

  (2) is not sent at the request of or with the express consent of the recipient.

       (c) An offense under this section is a Class C misdemeanor.

       (d) If conduct that constitutes an offense under this section also constitutes an offense under any other law, the actor may be prosecuted under this section or the other law.

the knowing transmission of visual material depicting images of any person engaging in sexual conduct, or the intimate parts of a person exposed, as well as the 'covered genitals of a male person that are in a discernibly turgid state'. This means the provision extends beyond penis images, and the sexual image distribution must occur without the 'express consent of the recipient'. The mental element is straightforward in requiring only intentional distribution without consent: there is, therefore, no specific motive requirement.

The Texan law will cover almost all cyberflashing cases: it is an offence of distribution, covers an extensive range of images, and has no motive restrictions. However, its wide definition of sexually explicit visual material means this provision, in effect, criminalises distributing pornography without consent. While this parallels longstanding recognition that unwelcome displays of pornography can constitute a hostile working environment, its breadth may give rise to legal challenges relating to over-criminalisation, and difficulties of enforcement.

California: The FLASH Act (Forbid Lewd Activity and Sexual Harassment)

In February 2020, Bumble also worked with legislators in California to introduce what is referred to as the FLASH Act (Forbid Lewd Activity and Sexual Harassment). Introducing the measure, Senator Connie Leyva stated: 'Cyber flashing – which primarily affects women – is a modern form of sexual harassment, and we have to put a stop to this inexcusable and offensive behavior' (Leyva, 2020). This measure involves knowingly sending an unsolicited image depicting various forms of sexual activity, or the 'exposed genitals or anus' of any person, by electronic means, subject to a $500 fine for a first time offence, rising to $1,000. The proposal is very clear in imposing the requirement that the recipient has 'expressly requested the image' and 'the request or consent is communicated in writing, including, but not limited to, a writing communicated by electronic means'.

As in Texas, these proposals stem from acknowledgement that existing laws on physical exposure do not encompass the new ways in which technology is being used to harass and abuse women. Conceptually, the measures understand the nature of cyberflashing, and recognise its commonality on dating apps and across social media. The proposed measures are wide in scope, and there is no motive requirement. Prosecution for this offence should, therefore, be straightforward, though it will be interesting to see whether the requirements on expressed consent make it into the final offence.

Pennsylvania: Unsolicited dissemination of 'lewd and lascivious' images

Pennsylvania is also considering measures similar to those in Texas. Referring to cyberflashing as an invasion of privacy (Coble, 2019) and a form of 'sexual harassment and … sexual assault' (Citizens Voice, 2019), the proposal is for a new sexual offence of 'unsolicited dissemination of intimate images' (House Bill No. 1974 of 2019 Session), with a fine of $300 and imprisonment of up to 90 days. The offence involves the knowing distribution of a 'sexually explicit image' where it has not been transmitted 'at the request of the recipient or with the express consent of the recipient'. The content covered is particularly broad, covering a 'lewd or lascivious visual depiction of a person's genitals, pubic area, breast or buttocks or nudity, if the nudity is depicted for the purpose of sexual stimulation or gratification of a person who might view the nudity'. The scope is limited by the requirement that the image is 'lewd or lascivious', but this does little to clarify the sorts of material under scrutiny.

New York: Sending unsolicited intimate images with intent to harass

In other parts of the US action is being taken and proposed at a more local level. For example, the City Council of New York has introduced measures challenging cyberflashing following campaigns raising awareness about its prevalence on public transport. The Council introduced legislation to discourage the practice, punishable by up to a year in jail, a $1,000 fine or both. The bipartisan effort aimed to 'raise awareness', remove the 'sense of impunity that may embolden those sending the images' (Otterman, 2018), and enhance 'public safety', connecting sexual exposure to the perpetration of other sexual offences (Gollayan, 2018).

The new provision amended the City Code to make it 'unlawful for a person, with the intent to harass, annoy or alarm another person, to send by electronic device an unsolicited intimate image' (Otterman, 2018). It covers distribution of an 'intimate image', including images of genitals, pubic area, the anus or engagement in sexual activity, thereby extending this provision beyond penis images, to a wide range of material. Nevertheless, the scope is limited by the need to prove the motive of causing alarm, annoyance or intending to harass.

The measure was adopted despite opposition from the New York Civil Liberties Union which claimed the measure would chill freedom of expression (City Council of New York, 2019). The organisation Brooklyn Defender Services also objected, warning criminalisation was 'more likely to ensnare young people than it is to deter this type of behaviour', that it was 'likely to lead to racially disparate enforcement' and that many young people may send unsolicited images in much the same way as a 'prank phone call' (Lee, 2019). While the 'prank' is unlikely to satisfy the motive requirements, the nature of policing and enforcement may mean that such nuance is missed. The organisation also objected on the basis that cyberflashing can be 'annoying and upsetting' but it is 'not so pernicious' such that it should be criminalised (Lee, 2019).

Chicago: AirDropping intimate images without consent

Similarly, Chicago City Council recently amended its Municipal Code, prohibiting cyberflashing on penalty of a $500 fine for a first offence, rising to up to 90 days in prison, community service, and a $1,000 fine (section 8-4-127). Included as part of the Code involving 'public peace and welfare', cyberflashing is defined as 'knowingly and without lawful justification sending an intimate image to another person through the use of data-dropping technology without the request or express consent of the person'.

The Chicago measure is both under and over-inclusive. The definition of 'intimate image' covers penis images, as well as images of a covered, erect penis, other genitals, and sexual activity. Conversely, the measure only applies to cyberflashing carried out through Bluetooth technologies, such as AirDrop, meaning that cyberflashing on social media or dating apps will not be covered. Moreover, the focus is unduly on the *means* of cyberflashing, rather than on its harms and non-consensual nature.

Cyberflashing: A global challenge

There are now even more countries seeking to target this behaviour. In Denmark, for example, the government recently raised the penalty for sending unsolicited penis images, with the maximum fine now being 5000 DKK (approx. US$760) (Mandua, 2020). Regions in Japan are also taking action against cyberflashers (Adelstein, 2019). In India, imaginative use of laws against pornography and 'insulting the modesty of a woman' have been deployed to successfully prosecute cyberflashing (Narayan, 2019), though such provisions raise other concerns about regulating women's conduct and freedom. And, in Finland, measures to criminalise cyberflashing are being considered, as a form of sexual harassment, and as part of an overhaul of its sexual offences (Guyoncourt, 2020). Many other countries, including Canada (Beattie, 2018) and Australia (Hopewell, 2014; Precel, 2019), with similar common law systems to England, also have various harassment and communications laws which could be used against cyberflashing. However, as with English law, this often requires considerable effort to shoe-horn cyberflashing into existing offences.

Conclusions

There are many valuable lessons to be learnt from this discussion. The Irish and Scottish examples show the value of broadly crafted sexual offences which are adaptable to new and changing means of perpetration. As these measures focused on other forms of offending – child-grooming in Scotland and indecency in Ireland – there remain limits and constraints in applying the offences to cyberflashing. Further, as the offences are largely unknown to cover cyberflashing, their expressive value is low, though this can be remedied by increasing awareness and use of the laws. Nonetheless, they point us towards the benefits of broader offences that are likely to stand the test of time.

In the absence of such general measures, other countries have opted for specific provisions targeting cyberflashing. This has many advantages, including clearly criminalising this behaviour, deploying the expressive power of the criminal law to signal that this is unwanted and unacceptable conduct, recognising the harms experienced by victim-survivors, and potentially supporting educational and other cyberflashing prevention initiatives. Singapore is instructive as the most focused provision, limiting its scope to images of genitals only, directly linking it to the offence of physical exposure, and clearly labelling it a sexual offence.

But lessons can still be drawn from the US states, where there are examples of both over- and under-inclusive provisions. These provisions generally have wide-ranging definitions of what constitutes the sexually explicit or 'lewd' material, meaning the measures apply to a wide range of porno-graphic materials. This naturally follows from understanding cyberflashing as a form of sexual harassment, and mirrors workplace sexual harassment laws. It also avoids some tortuous evidential requirements. However, it does risk being overly-broad, and thus might encounter considerable opposition. In contrast, provisions introduced as public safety measures unduly limit the scope to cyberflashing carried out over Bluetooth and similar technologies. The following chapter takes forward these discussions, examining the options of specific targeted offences, as well as broader provisions covering more forms of sexual intrusion.

SIX

Criminalising Cyberflashing: Recommendations for Law Reform

I would still feel more safe with a law.
(Natalie, quoted in Gallagher, 2018a)

I would completely support [a law] and think it is absolutely necessary … We need women to feel safe in public spaces and this will be a crucial step forward.
(Jenny, quoted in Gallagher, 2018a)

Cyberflashing is a sexual intrusion that infringes sexual autonomy and can induce significant harms. For these reasons, we have argued that there is a role for the criminal law in targeting cyberflashing so that victim-survivors' voices are heard, their experiences recognised and there are effective means to prosecute offenders and seek redress. In addition, the criminal law can provide a valuable normative foundation for prevention and education initiatives.

Accordingly, this chapter recommends a bespoke offence specifically criminalising cyberflashing and we set out the key criteria to be considered in any such reform. As well as this specific crime, we raise the possibility of a broader sexual offence that would encompass cyberflashing, as well as a wider range of abusive and intrusive practices. We suggest that the potential of such a reform needs to be considered in the context of a much-needed review of the scope and reach of sexual offence laws more generally, taking into account the changing nature of perpetration, particularly advancing technology and online abuse.

Targeting cyberflashing: Crafting a bespoke offence

The major benefit in an offence directly targeting cyberflashing is that its expressive function will be to the fore. The expressive function plays two particular roles, the first being prevention. It makes it known that these behaviours are now considered wrong, potentially harmful and consequently are being made subject to society's most coercive state power, the criminal law. Together with campaigns and other public awareness-raising measures, this may begin to shift norms and aid prevention initiatives. In short, it may become less acceptable to send unsolicited penis images. Second, naming this harm and taking steps to prevent and punish it, gives victim-survivors a sense of hermeneutical justice: they are now better understood, their experiences now recognised; they are not alone.

As well as these expressive functions, a bespoke new law also offers more options for redress. Being clear about what behaviour is now being targeted may encourage both reporting and active investigations. Further, if reports are made, prosecutions may be more straightforward. While we canvass options for a general offence covering many forms of sexual intrusion, the downside of such an option is that prosecutions rely on interpretations as to what constitutes factors such as harm, threats, coercion, intrusion, abuse or similar behaviours. The concern is that such criteria may not be interpreted – by victims, criminal justice personnel and judges – to include cyberflashing. The benefit, therefore, of an offence which directly addresses the conduct is that we do not then have to try to convince others than cyberflashing may indeed be threatening, abusive, harmful or whatever other terms determine the scope of the offence. Nonetheless, we can only realise the benefits of a bespoke law if that pro-vision is carefully crafted and effective, covering the variety and complexity of cyberflashing. We set out here some of the key components of any such reform.

Cyberflashing as a sexual offence

We suggested in earlier chapters that cyberflashing is a sexual intrusion which infringes sexual autonomy, and the criminal law must recognise it as such. This framing as a sexual crime is vital to ensuring proper recognition of the experiences and harms of many victim-survivors, as well as effectively shaping education and prevention initiatives. In addition to underpinning the expressive and educative role of the law, this conceptual framing also impacts on the law's practical enforcement. Sexual offences, for example, usually entitle victim-survivors to specific rights and protections, such as anonymity on reporting and special protections in court processes (Rook and Ward, 2016). Such offences may also be directed through the criminal justice system in particular ways, for example being processed by specially trained police and criminal justice personnel, and have an appropriate range of sentencing options, including sexual harm prevention orders where suitable. Any new cyberflashing offence, therefore, should be characterised as a sexual offence, following countries such as Singapore and Texas.

All the penises: Not limited to images of the perpetrator's genitals

The nature of the images included in any new offence will be a key factor in determining its effectiveness. We have defined cyberflashing as the unsolicited distribution of penis images, as this phenomenon centres on men sharing penis images, rather than women sending images of their genitals. It is also the penis image which, for some victim-survivors, conveys the sense of threat and abuse. In principle, therefore, a cyberflashing offence might only extend to penis images. There would be some justification for this, as a review prior to the Sexual Offences Act 2003 concluded that while there was a need for an amended offence of sexual exposure, there was no reason to extend this to disclosure of female genitalia, as this was not a common occurrence and, in practice, does not carry the same degree of threat or potential harm (Home Office, 2000, para 8.2.8). Further, while female exposure of genitalia can be part of a pattern of sexual offending, it was considered that such behaviour was more likely to be part of a wider 'abusive situation' and of a different order to what is usually considered indecent exposure, and therefore best dealt with through other sexual offences (Home Office, 2000, para 8.2.8). The focus, therefore, was on the potential harms and threats of the deliberate and targeted exposure of the penis.

However, non-discrimination and gender neutrality were key principles at the heart of reform efforts, meaning that the exposure offence refers to 'genitals' (Home Office, 2002). These principles continue to inform reform debates and we suggest, therefore, that a new offence should cover 'genital' images for reasons of principle (and comparability with the exposure offence), as well as to ensure pragmatically that the focus of public debate is on the harms and key aspects of reform, rather than on the exclusion of vulvas from the legislation. While technically the offence will be one applying to genitals, cyberflashing is known to be about unsolicited penis images; the reality remains that the 'problem' to be tackled is the sending of penis images without consent.

That said, we do not think an offence should be limited to images of the perpetrator's own penis. For example, in a paradigmatically threatening scenario where a woman receives an unsolicited penis image while alone on public transport, her fear is not dependent on her sure knowledge that the penis in the image belongs to the perpetrator. Indeed, she may not know who sent her the image. To require proof that it is the perpetrator's penis in the image neglects to understand the nature of the experience and harm.

Further, requiring proof that it is the perpetrator's penis would institute a prosecutorial hurdle that is, to all extents and purposes, insurmountable. If all a perpetrator must do to halt a prosecution is to declare that the penis in the image is not his, there will be few prosecutions indeed. Proof that a penis belongs to a particular person is not only technically extremely difficult (Irish Legal News, 2018; Mair, 2018) but even if the technology became available, it would likely be hardly ever used, if at all, in view of the fact that similar techniques identifying hands in child sexual abuse cases are only used in a small number of cases (Benson, 2017; Mair, 2018). Such a requirement, therefore, will prove such a practical disincentive to further investigation as to render any offence almost redundant.

However, the English Law Commission has warned against an 'overly broad' offence if it includes all penis images (Law Commission, 2020, paras 6.148 and 6.139). In particular, they suggest that sending a publicly available image of a naked person (including their genitalia) to an acquaintance who knows that the image is not that of the sender is of a 'different order of threat' to where a stranger sends a penis image (Law Commission, 2020, paras 6.139 – 6.140). They conclude that the harm, therefore, of cyberflashing is not a function of whose genitals are in the image but a 'more nuanced question of context and the apprehension of the recipient' and that any new law should, therefore, be more constrained and limited to the perpetrator's own penis (Law Commission, 2020, para 6.139).

Harm is indeed context specific and different forms of cyberflashing will induce varying harms, depending on the circumstances. However, while it is possible that the acquaintance's experiences are less harmful than if a stranger were to receive the image, this may not always or necessarily be the case. Accordingly, we are not convinced that such a possible scenario should dictate the reach of the law (McGlynn and Johnson, 2020). Rather, the egregious harms which may be experienced should loom large in our choices over the scope of any provisions. Further, in practical terms, if there is no harm experienced in this acquaintance scenario, there will be no report to the police or subsequent investigation. On balance, therefore, we maintain that a cyberflashing offence should not be limited to images of the perpetrator's own penis.

It may be that proposals limiting an offence to images of a perpetrator's own penis assume that motivations for cyberflashing are similar to those associated with physical exposure, namely the sexual dysfunction of exhibitionism, with often predatory consequences and a precursor to other forms of sexual offending (Hanmer and Saunders, 1984; McNeill, 1987; Green, 2018). Viewed from this perspective, the problem to be addressed in legislation is indeed the individual exposing his *own* penis, with the fear of escalating sexual offending. However, such an understanding of physical exposure neither captures the full extent of 'flashing' motivations (Hanmer and Saunders, 1984; McNeill, 1987; Green, 2018), nor of cyberflashing, with its wide-ranging purposes as discussed in previous chapters. It would be a real concern if this approach to understanding cyberflashing dominated law reform proposals.

Fake images and imaginary people

It is not uncommon when sharing intimate images to enhance or alter them, practises that are ever easier as technology advances (Chesney and Citron, 2019), and this is no less the case with penis images (Scott, 2020). This advancing technology has given rise to considerable concern in relation to the non-consensual distribution of intimate images, where many laws that criminalise these practices in principle do not extend to altered images, leaving victim-survivors with little redress (McGlynn et al, 2019; Eaton and McGlynn, 2020; Henry et al, 2020). In the cyberflashing context, therefore, we must ensure that laws can deal with advancing technology and cover images that are altered and enhanced. An offence, for example, that relies on proof that the offender sent an image of his own penis must not be inoperative simply because he has used digital technology to enhance or alter that image.

As discussed in earlier chapters, the Scottish offence of coercing someone to look at a sexual image provides that the image can be of the offender, another person or an 'imaginary person'. Similarly, Scots law on the non-consensual sharing of intimate images extends to material modified by digital or other means (Chalmers and Leverick, 2017; McGlynn, 2019). These provisions ensure that the law is keeping pace with digital technologies which are making it easier to create images where it is almost impossible to tell whether they are 'real' or 'faked'. English law lags far behind in this regard and future laws must ensure that they apply to altered images if offences are to have any real impact or effect.

Target distribution not actual viewing of images

A bespoke offence should target the distribution of the image and not require actual viewing. We have seen in earlier chapters that the Scots offence is one of causing the victim to view the image, compared with the Singaporean and Texan focus on simple distribution. The Scottish approach is obviously more challenging to prove, introducing an unnecessary threshold. To be preferred, therefore, is the more straightforward focus on distribution, particularly important in cyberflashing cases where the victim-survivor may not see the actual image, or the proof that they did is difficult to secure.

The problem with motives

In determining what needs to be proven of the perpetrator's intentions and state of mind, there are broadly two options, focusing either on malign motives or on acting without con-sent, with some offences including both. The Singaporean cyberflashing offence, for example, requires proof of either intention to cause distress and alarm, or of sexual gratification (as well as proof of non-consent).

The English Law Commission has recommended an offence based on proof of motive to cause distress or alarm, rather than non-consent (Law Commission, 2020, paras 6.128–6.133; McGlynn and Johnson, 2020). However, when we consider the criminal law as a whole, motive requirements are 'exceptional' (Franks, 2017; Ormerod and Laird, 2018, 101) and this applies equally to sexual offences where the focus is usually on non-consent and the motive is deemed irrelevant to the harm inflicted (McGlynn, 2018). This approach is based on the longstanding idea that the motive for the potentially criminal act is irrelevant: for instance, theft in order to feed one's starving children is still theft regardless of the commendable motive.

As well as being uncommon, motive requirements are also particularly difficult to prove as they require an investigation into the mind of the perpetrator that is even more difficult than demonstrating intention to carry out a specific act (Candeub, 1994). Proof of motive often relies on reasoning by analogy to try to understand what is in the mind of the person; that is, what would we do in such situations or what would we think (Candeub, 1994). This may make some sense, or is certainly easier, in relation to common actions – such as throwing a punch in a fight. But it becomes much more complex and questionable where the experiences differ from everyday encounters, such as cyberflashing which is a relatively new behaviour and common only among certain groups. In addition, where motives are determined by drawing on the norms of those investigating or judging the conduct, the effectiveness of laws covering unfamiliar or gendered activities such as cyberflashing can be called into question.

The other way in which motive might be evidenced is by associated behaviour, such as accompanying comments, actions or text. Again, though, this raises problems for practices such as cyberflashing where there is often little other accompanying behaviour, words or conduct. Determining the state of mind of the actor, therefore, is evidentially challenging, acting as a serious disincentive to prosecution.

And, indeed, we can see these concerns playing out in areas of law related to cyberflashing. Motive requirements are included, for example, in image-based sexual abuse provisions – such as English law's requirement to demonstrate the motive to cause distress (McGlynn and Rackley, 2017; Eaton and McGlynn, 2020). This requirement has been roundly criticised for limiting the scope of the offences and hindering prosecutions (Franks, 2017; North Yorkshire Police Fire and Crime Commissioner, 2018; McGlynn et al, 2019; Eaton and McGlynn, 2020; Henry et al, 2020). In particular, by privileging particular motives such as 'revenge', not only are many common motivations excluded, particularly where offenders act to enhance their status among friends, but the expressive role of the law is constrained by suggesting that only acts with the specified motives are harmful. As Mary Ann Franks (2017, 1289) argues, imposing motive requirements results in 'arbitrary distinctions' between perpetrators. In addition, the evidence suggests that police and prosecutors are more reluctant to take forward cases due to challenges of proving the distress motive (Law Commission, 2018, para 10.107; North Yorkshire Police Fire and Crime Commissioner, 2018; McGlynn et al, 2019). Therefore, requiring specific purposes to be proven not only fails to recognise the complexity of perpetrator motives and the nature of the abuse, but it also inhibits and limits prosecutions.

This is not to suggest that motive is irrelevant. It plays an important role in evidentiary terms, for the simple reason that the prosecution is more likely to convince adjudicators of guilt if they supply a tenable motive. Similarly, motive will be relevant to sentencing. But this is substantially different from requiring proof of motive as an element of the crime. It may well be challenging to get investigators and adjudicators to infer that the offender had the required motive from the circumstances of sending an unsolicited penis image, particularly if they consider cyberflashing to be relatively harmless. In addition, the sender seeking to make contact for sexual/dating purposes may genuinely have no intention to cause distress, or quite possibly no awareness of the risk of causing distress, though is still acting without consent. Motive requirements, therefore, do not address the full range of cyberflashing practices and, in focusing on the possible ends being sought by perpetrators (such as distress) rather than the wrongful act (sending without consent), may seriously limit the impact of any new law.

Nonetheless, if motives are to be required, they should at least be as broad as possible, and as well as causing distress and alarm, humiliation should also be included, as this is a harm reported by some victim-survivors. It also follows Scots law on coercing someone to view a sexual image and English law on 'upskirting' (Gillespie, 2019). As discussed in earlier chapters, humiliation is understood as lowering someone's dignity or self-respect and can therefore extend the scope to include actions aimed at shaming, demeaning or degrading the victim-survivor (Gillespie, 2019). Humiliation also has a close connection to international understandings of sexual harassment where creating a 'hostile, intimidating, degrading or humiliating environment' is to be prohibited (Istanbul Convention, 2011).

As well as extending the range of motives required, the scope of the law can be strengthened by covering not only a direct intention to cause distress (or other motive), but also an awareness by the accused of the risk that their actions could cause these outcomes. This would mean that those who decide to act for one purpose, such as gaining status with their friends, but who are also aware that they may cause distress, alarm or humiliation, would fall within the offence. While such changes would not cover all eventualities, they would constitute important improvements.

Non-consent as the core wrong

The alternative to focusing on motives is to start from the core wrong of the offending conduct, namely non-consent.

The problem is not the distribution of penis images per se, nor only distribution for particular purposes, but distribution *without consent*. The essence of cyberflashing is intrusive sexual behaviour: the person receiving the images neither asked for them, nor received them with consent. The non-consensual act breaches the victim-survivor's sexual autonomy, regardless of whether the perpetrator intended a particular harm and regardless of whether the act did indeed cause that specific harm. A cyberflashing offence, therefore, should focus on knowledge of the lack of consent as the mental element to be proven, as in many US states, as discussed in previous chapters.

However, while this approach has conceptual resonance, it encounters two main challenges, namely the practical difficulties of proving non-consent and concerns that consent sets the threshold for criminality too low. First, in practice, proving non-consent in sexual offences is fraught with difficulties, leading to many cases being dismissed. Problems arise in determining the state of mind of the victim-survivor – did they consent and how is that proven – which, in turn, commonly leads to a focus on the victim's behaviour (Gore, 2020). In cyberflashing, where images are sent to a stranger, proof of non-consent should be relatively straightforward. In other cases, and in the absence of express agreement, offenders may make claims, for example, that the complainant had previously welcomed penis images either from the offender or others and therefore he thought there was consent. While this does not demonstrate consent in the particular instance, such reasoning and evidence is often used in making claims of reasonable belief in consent (as provided for in English sexual offence laws) (Rook and Ward, 2016). Perhaps more tangential would be a claim that participating in a particular dating app, for example, implied consent to receiving penis images as that is commonplace on that particular app. While such a claim should not stand scrutiny, the risk is that such assertions are sufficient to inhibit victim-survivors from reporting to the police, or the police and prosecutors pursuing a case.

Some mitigation of these concerns could be made by statutory detail on what may or may not constitute consent, such as the Scottish provisions on non-consensual sharing of intimate images which state that consent must be 'specific to the particular disclosure' (section 2(4) Abusive Behaviour and Sexual Harm (Scotland) Act 2016). Translated into this context, that might mean a provision stating that consent must be to the particular distribution, not to receiving penis images or pornographic material in general.

To an extent, these problems are recognised in some of the US provisions which mandate proof of consent, precluding any implied consent, such as the Californian proposals discussed in earlier chapters which require the recipient to have 'expressly' requested the image. More generally, it is such concerns that are behind sexual offence laws focusing on 'affirmative consent' models which require evidence of positive behaviours demonstrating consent (Burgin, 2018). Still, while the US provisions underline the significance of consent, and that it cannot be assumed or implied, they also create their own challenges in potentially criminalising consensual conduct where there is an absence of evidence of 'express' or written agreement, but there was in fact consent.

This leads to the second concern with a consent-based offence, that it may be too far-reaching. For example, the English Law Commission suggest that where someone in a 'loving relationship' sends an image of their genitalia to their partner without consent, and where certainly there was no express consent, this should not meet a 'threshold for criminality' (Law Commission, 2020, para 1.148; McGlynn and Johnson, 2020). While it may be that in such a scenario there are no consequential harms experienced by the partner, it remains the case that this was non-consensual sexual conduct. The *wrong* therefore of cyberflashing has been committed, even if there are no demonstrable harms. Holding on to the core wrong in sexual offending is important if we are to refrain from only legislating where there is evidence of consequential harms, or only where an individual victim can prove they have experienced harm.

Further, it seems that the Law Commission's hypothetical example rests on assumptions about types of relationships, and assumptions around lack of harm, that may not be borne out in practice. Even in 'loving relationships' consent should be sought for sexual activity and while it might be assumed here that sending a penis image carries a low risk of harm, this may not always be the case. It is not difficult to imagine situations where being sent a penis image, without warning, may not be experienced as 'loving', but concerning and potentially threatening. In addition, if we were to shape the law around this example and assume there will never be any harm, we risk denying protection, recognition and redress to those who do not experience receipt of the penis image in the ways imagined.

Another way of considering this issue is to think about whether we focus on the cases involving significant harms that are currently without redress, ensuring that they both come within the scope of the law, and are realistically prosecutable, even if this means drafting a law of potentially broad application. Or, do we seek to draft a law that ensures all borderline or difficult cases are excluded, even if this risks omitting potentially harmful cases? In making such determinations, it may be instructive to examine similar crimes.

Consider, for example, offences covering the non-consensual distribution of intimate images. There may be cases where an intimate image is shared without consent but for a potentially benign motive, such as for amusement, and the person affected experiences no harm, as they are not bothered by the image being shared without their agreement and indeed, they may even welcome it (Henry et al, 2020, 6). Technically, these actions would constitute a criminal offence in many jurisdictions (despite the benign motive and victim satisfaction) because the distribution is made without consent, regardless of the particular motives (though not English law which also requires proof of intention to cause distress) (McGlynn and Rackley, 2017; Crofts and Kirchengast, 2019; Henry et al, 2020).

Such laws have balanced the different interests at play and have chosen not to limit the offence to either proof of particular motives or actual harm to the victim, because to do so would fail to capture the real harms of these actions and hinder prosecutions (though there are defences in some jurisdictions based on reasonable grounds for acting, see Crofts and Kirchengast, 2019). This path has been chosen because there is still a wrongful act: the privacy and sexual autonomy of the person in the image has been breached. As the Australian Senate Legal and Constitutional Affairs References Committee (2016, 51) stated when reviewing these offences, consent should 'be the central tenet of any non-consensual sharing of intimate images offences'. The emphasis, therefore, is on the significance of the wrong of non-consensual conduct in sexual contexts. Further, in the sort of case identified by the Law Commission, with benign motives and an unharmed victim, in practice, prosecutions are unlikely as there will be no police report and no public interest in pursuing any such case.

This example does, however, show that ambiguity and difficult cases are perhaps unavoidable. The issue is where the balance lies. The English Law Commission has recommended limiting the offence, partly because they propose a fall-back option of a communications offence which may cover some cyberflashing cases (Law Commission, 2020, para 5.49). However, while there are real concerns with consent-based provisions, this should not lead us to adopt laws which are otherwise flawed or less effective. The problems with consent in sexual offences lie in problematic cultural and societal assumptions about sexual activity, sexual double standards and myths about rape (Gray, 2015; Larcombe et al, 2016; Burgin, 2018). These difficulties are not a failure in the substantive law per se, but in how the laws are understood, interpreted and put into practice. The focus for change should, therefore, be on social and cultural attitudes, rather than, in effect, accepting such attitudes as immutable and rewriting our laws in response.

Accordingly, notwithstanding the problems with consent-based provisions, we suggest non-consent as the foundation of a bespoke cyberflashing law, as this constitutes the core wrong of the behaviour. One of the main reasons for adopting a specific offence is its expressive value, bringing to public attention the phenomenon and harms of what is known as 'cyberflashing'. Centring non-consent better recognises victim-survivors' experiences, providing them with a form of hermeneutical justice, whereby their experiences are known, understood and recognised. It also underscores the links with other forms of sexual offending, abuse and harassment, including online activities where consent to send and receive images is emphasised.

Criminalisation, unsolicited penis images and same-sex attracted men

On the other hand, due to the pervasiveness of unsolicited penis imagery in some online interactions among same-sex attracted men, there have been concerns that criminalising cyberflashing would impose a heteronormative framework onto some men's communications, amounting to an 'attack' on gay techno-cultures (Dawson, 2019). Specifically, and referring to recent legislation in Texas, concerns have been raised that prosecuting men in this context could inadvertently 'out' people and put their personal safety at risk. Further:

> The crackdown does seem beneficial for those who follow a heteronormative timeline of personal sexual experiences … but there is a dichotomy when it comes to straight vs gay culture of sexual partnership … Gay culture is born from suppression … we resort to finding sexual partners through shared glances at a bar, something that needs an on-the-spot response, which I guess

has now been digitally translated into sending a picture
of my hole and waiting for a yes or a no.

(Dawson, 2019)

While this raises significant issues, and emphasises the
importance for any cyberflashing prosecutions being propor-
tionate and in the public interest, we simultaneously argue
that the experience and implications of being sent unsolicited
penis images in a same-sex dating context must nevertheless
be viewed as non-prescriptive, and instead requires nuanced
contextual analysis (Paasonen et al, 2019). It is important to
note that just because unsolicited penis images are prevalent and often framed as a 'sexual cultural practice' in some
online same-sex dating and hook-up contexts, it does not
mean that this is a unanimously welcomed interaction. For
example, Light (2016) found that some same-sex platform
users choose not to engage with profiles that have a penis
as a profile image and are 'wary' of them. Others suggest
even in online contexts where unsolicited penis images are
normalised and/or expected, 'if certain lines are crossed,
certain measures should be taken' (Dawson, 2019). This
underscores the value of the wrong of cyberflashing being
recognised in all cases where penis images are sent without
the recipient's consent.

Criminalising sexual intrusions

While we have emphasised the benefits of a specific
cyberflashing offence, there are, however, some downsides.
Specific offences often follow paradigmatic cases raised in
public debates, with the result that subsequent legislation solely
or predominantly focusses on such examples. For example, laws
on non-consensual distribution of intimate images have been
introduced in many countries but have too often focussed on
the 'revenge porn' narrative, thereby criminalising only some
forms of this abuse (McGlynn and Rackley, 2017; Henry et al,

2020). In a similar vein, such offences have tended to concentrate on the distribution of a particular (unaltered) image without consent, not foreseeing that technology would enable modification of images to make them pornographic with largely the same effect (Chesney and Citron, 2019; McGlynn et al, 2019).

Indeed, this focus on a particular image also means that while a law on non-consensual distribution of images might well apply to cyberflashing, such laws generally do not, as legislation focuses on the non-consent of the person featured in the image. A similarly myopic approach can be seen in recent English legislation on 'upskirting' which requires an image to be taken 'beneath' someone's clothing which does mirror paradigmatic examples of 'upskirting', but this specificity excludes other invasive images (Gillespie, 2019).

What these examples reveal is that a dedicated focus on paradigmatic examples of a particular practice can lead to laws that, while covering some forms of the abusive behaviours, risk excluding others, particularly new means of perpetration. They also demonstrate the tendency for very specific types of behaviours to be at the forefront of legal categorisation and analysis, particularly the mode of perpetration, rather than the nature of the harms and impacts (Wegerstad, 2021). In sum, therefore, the risk with a specific cyberflashing offence is that while it may cover the forms of sexual intrusion of which we are currently aware, perhaps before too long, we will discover its limitations, as perpetrators find ever new ways of abusing and harassing others.

Another option, therefore, is to develop a law which has more general applicability. The principal advantage of introducing such an offence is that it would help to future-proof the law so that it can cover new ways and means of perpetrating abuse. To consider the possibilities of such measures, we examine Swedish and Irish provisions which cover a wide range of different sexual intrusions, as well as an option put forward by the Law Commission in Hong Kong.

Sweden's criminalisation of 'sexual molestation'

When considering a more general offence that will capture cyberflashing, Sweden provides an instructive example (Wegerstad, 2021). Sweden's catch-all provision of 'sexual molestation/harassment' covers acts not otherwise included in more specific offences such as rape. This offence encompasses 'a person who exposes themselves to another person in a manner that is liable to cause discomfort, or who otherwise molests a person by word or deed in a way that is liable to violate that person's sexual integrity' (Wegerstad, 2021). This is a sexual offence, and the aim is to protect 'sexual integrity' and sexual self-determination, with a maximum term of imprisonment of two years.

As Wegerstad (2021) explains, this provision could encompass most forms of intrusive sexist behaviour and therefore fits well with a continuum understanding of the nature of sexual abuse. It covers physical and verbal intrusions, if the behaviour violates the person's sexual integrity, and therefore has been applied to cyberflashing. It also covered a man repeatedly, in a public place, asked a young woman to have sex with him in exchange for money, as well as the practice of upskirting (Wegerstad, 2021). These examples demonstrate that this provision manages to cover a range of intrusive behaviours, many of which are not often included in sexual offence laws. However, the law is subject to a range of limitations established in the case law, such as where a male manager touching the inside of the clothed thigh of a woman trainee was considered inappropriate and unwelcome, but not behaviour of such a clear sexual nature as to be criminalised (Wegerstad, 2021).

This latter example demonstrates the fluidity of concepts such as sexual assault, intrusion or molestation, because while this case was excluded from Swedish law, it would most likely constitute sexual assault in English law because of the physical element, even though English law would not cover many of the other forms of conduct covered by the provision. This emphasises the challenges of a more open-ended provision where the boundaries of criminal conduct are not always clear and may require litigation, as well as the development of adequate policing and prosecution practices. The benefits of breadth and future-proofing the law need to be balanced against a more uncertain understanding of the scope and applicability of the law.

Hong Kong: Sexual acts causing fear, degradation or harm

A similar measure was proposed, though not adopted, by the Hong Kong Law Reform Commission in 2012 (2012, para 6.26) which recommended expanding the law on sexual assault to 'cover any act of a sexual nature which would have been likely to cause another person "fear, degradation or harm" had it been known to the other person'. Specifically, they recommended an offence where a person (A) who, without the consent of another person (B) and without a reasonable belief that B consents, intentionally does an act of a sexual nature which would have been likely to cause B fear, degradation or harm had it been known to B, irrespective of whether it was known to B (Law Reform Commission of Hong Kong, 2012, 94).

Interestingly, this proposal arose out of concerns that the existing law did not cover 'upskirting'. The Commission stated that its proposal would acknowledge 'the sexual nature of such activity and the need for respect for sexual autonomy' and that such an expansion in the scope of sexual assault was justified because it is 'a violation of another person's sexual autonomy' (Law Reform Commission of Hong Kong, 2012, paras 6.25–6.28). In the end, the measure was not adopted, with more recent proposals on upskirting being far more limited in their scope and drafted to cover only the very specific behaviour of upskirting and voyeurism (Hong Kong Law Reform Commission, 2019).

Ireland: 'Offensive conduct of a sexual nature'

As discussed in earlier chapters, a similar offence applies in Ireland where a person 'intentionally engages in offensive conduct of a sexual nature' which is defined as 'any behaviour of a sexual nature which, having regard to all the circumstances, is likely to cause fear, distress or alarm to any person who is, or might reasonably be expected to be, aware of any such behaviour' (section 45 of the Criminal Law (Sexual Offences) Act 2017). While this offence does not specifically require proof of non-consent, it does require behaviour the intention of which is to cause fear or distress, which suggests no consent from the recipient. While the Irish provision employs the problematic language of 'offensive' conduct, as opposed to harmful or non-consensual conduct, the definition itself does not require or extend to 'offensive' conduct in terms of it being morally repugnant.

Reviewing sexual offence laws

While each of these more general offences have much to commend them, the boundaries and specific requirements should be considered as part of a broader evaluation of sexual offence laws and possible reforms. Such a review can begin to consider the role of the substantive law in creating or sustaining the 'justice gap' in rape and sexual assault cases (Lonsway and Archambault, 2012; Hohl and Stanko, 2015). It should also examine the shifting means of perpetrating abuse, and the changing nature of sexual offending, particularly due to advancing technology and online behaviours (Henry and Powell, 2016; Powell and Henry, 2017). It would also be timely to re-assess why sexual offending takes place, and how that shapes the substantive law; this is particularly relevant with the increasing use of motive requirements in sexual offences laws and technological advances making it far easier to perpetrate crimes, as well as changing the nature of the offending conduct.

In addition, assumptions that sexual offending is motivated purely by sexual arousal continue to plague reform discussions, despite evidence being clear that offending is motivated by a complex interplay of power, control, entitlement and punishment, as well as sexual gratification (Mann and Hollin, 2007; Fulu et al, 2013; McGlynn, 2018). It would also be an opportune time to review sentencing and punishment options, extending the range of possibilities to more rehabilitative and educational measures. Each of these elements of a review would feed into discussion of the scope and nature of a broad offence of sexual intrusion.

In particular, such a review may highlight areas not currently covered by the substantive law but which would suitably be included in a broader offence of sexual intrusion, such as some forms of street harassment (Tran, 2015; Vera-Gray, 2017a; 2018) including instances of physical exposure not currently included in the Sexual Offences Act 2003. A sexual intrusion offence may also extend to forms of image-based sexual abuse not currently covered by the criminal law, such as non-consensual distribution of intimate images motivated by purposes other than distress or harm (McGlynn et al, 2019); or 'cum tributes', where a man has ejaculated over a person's image (not necessarily nude or sexual) and then posted that material online (Rogers, 2016). The boundaries would need to be carefully considered due to the possibility of such an offence including non-consensual distribution of pornographic materials more generally. Therefore, a review should also examine laws relating to pornography (Vera-Gray and McGlynn, 2020), and their overlap with sexual offences.

Conclusions

We have seen throughout this book that the current criminal law in England and Wales is failing victim-survivors, and society generally. Accordingly, we recommend adopting a specific criminal offence to directly challenge this practice.

The introduction of a targeted offence – when followed by widespread and effective awareness-raising campaigns – has the benefit of ensuring a greater likelihood that the offending conduct is subject to criminal sanction, in that victim-survivors and criminal justice personnel will all be more aware of its existence. If well-crafted, a specific offence will also facilitate prosecutions as the harms and wrongful nature of the conduct is already determined, rather than being subject to the vagaries of individual judgments on its potential harms.

Despite the advantages of a bespoke offence, there will be practical difficulties in prosecuting such offences. For example, the perpetrator is often unknown (Bowden, 2020; Gallagher, 2020). In addition, there is often no proof of the distribution of the image (as the victim deletes or 'declines' it). Further, if an offence is limited to images of the perpetrator's own penis, this will constitute a virtually insurmountable barrier to prosecution.

In any event, as we have emphasised, such practical constraints should not limit our ambition for a criminal law that sanctions wrongful, non-consensual conduct infringing an individual's sexual autonomy. As a sexual intrusion which is potentially harmful, there remain benefits in deploying the criminal law, including its expressive and symbolic role, not only in sending a message to society in general and to potential perpetrators, but importantly to victim-survivors in terms of society's recognition of their harms and experiences. Further, some victim-survivors may choose to report to the police, even where they are aware that little may happen, for the same reasons that other sexual violence survivors have done so, as a form of 'symbolic protest' (Taylor and Norma, 2011) or to try to protect others (Brooks-Hay, 2020).

While this expressive power of law may be deployed in many different circumstances and for varied purposes, in relation to cyberflashing and other forms of technology-facilitated abuse, the time has never been better for action. With technology developing, and as awareness grows of the problems and harms of cyberflashing, we have the chance to (re)establish and (re)define the norms by which society views and addresses this phenomenon. Accordingly, while we must continue to be alive to law's contradictions, unforeseen consequences and capacity to oppress, introducing a law to tackle cyberflashing may encourage greater awareness of the harms of cyberflashing, contribute to victim-survivors' sense of justice and recognition of their experiences, and shape prevention and change initiatives. It is time to listen to victim-survivors of cyberflashing and take their experiences and perspectives as the foundation for a new law criminalising cyberflashing. It is time for fundamental change.

References

Amnesty International. (2017) 'Amnesty reveals alarming impact of online abuse against women', www.amnesty.org/en/latest/news/2017/11/amnesty-reveals-alarming-impact-of-online-abuse-against-women/

Amundsen, Rikke. (2020) '"A male dominance kind of vibe": Approaching unsolicited dick pics as sexism', *New Media and Society*, 20(3): 1085–1102.

Are, Carolina. (2020) 'How Instagram's algorithm is censoring women and vulnerable users but helping online abusers', *Feminist Media Studies*, 20(5): 741–744.

Arnold, Michael. (2003) 'On the phenomenology of technology: The "Janus-faces" of mobile phones', *Information and Organization*, 13(4): 231–256.

Auchmuty, Rosemary and van Marle, Karin. (2012) 'Special issue: Carol Smart's feminism and the power of law', *Feminist Legal Studies*, 20: 65–69.

Australian Senate Legal and Constitutional Affairs References Committee. (2016) 'Phenomenon colloquially referred to as "revenge porn"', www.aph.gov.au/Parliamentary_Business/Committees/Senate/Legal_and_Constitutional_Affairs/Revenge_porn/Report

Barr, Caelainn. (2019) 'Why are rape prosecutions at a 10-year low?', *The Guardian*, 12 September, www.theguardian.com/society/2019/sep/12/why-are-rape-prosecutions-at-a-10-year-low-england-wales

Bowden, Emma. (2020) 'Cyberflashing on trains "largely unreported"', *YahooNews*, 19 February.

Bumble. (nd) 'Why Bumble backed a new law to curb online sexual harassment', https://bumble.com/the-buzz/lewd-photo-texas-law

BBC News. (2019) 'Government vows to protect women from unwanted penis photos', 6 March, www.bbc.co.uk/news/uk-politics-47474336

BBC News. (2020) 'New Yorker fires Jeffrey Toobin for exposing himself on Zoom', 11 November, www.bbc.co.uk/news/world-us-canada-54912610

Beattie, Samantha. (2018) 'Canada's laws can't handle "Cyberflashing", a new type of sexual harassment', *Huffington Post*, 13 December, www.huffingtonpost.ca/2018/12/13/cyberflashing-canada-airdrop-dick-pics-subway-sexual-harassment_a_23617459/

Beaty, Zoe. (2019) 'Why the UK needs to take cyber-flashing seriously?', *The Times*, 8 December, www.thetimes.co.uk/edition/style/why-the-uk-needs-to-take-cyber-flashing-seriously-73c0r02f9

Beebeejaun, Yasminah. (2017) 'Gender, urban space, and the right to everyday life', *Journal of Urban Affairs*, 39(3): 323–334.

Bell, Sarah. (2015) 'Police investigate "first cyber-flashing" case', *BBC News*, 13 August, www.bbc.co.uk/news/technology-33889225

Bennetto, Jason. (1995) 'Victims of flashing "perceive threat of rape or murder"', *The Independent*, 24 July, www.independent.co.uk/news/victims-of-flashing-perceive-threat-of-rape-or-murder-1592974.html

Benson, Richard. (2017) 'To catch a paedophile, you only need to look at their hands', *Wired*, 20 September, www.wired.co.uk/article/sue-black-forensics-hand-markings-paedophiles-rapists

Bernstein, Elizabeth. (2005) 'Militarised humanitarianism meets carceral feminism: the politics of sex, rights and freedom in contemporary antitrafficking campaigns', *Signs*, 36(1): 45–71.

Bernstein, Elizabeth. (2012) 'Carceral politics as gender justice? The "traffic in women" and neoliberal circuits of crime, sex and rights', *Theory and Society*, 41: 233–259.

Bond, Emma and Tyrrell, Katie. (2018) 'Understanding revenge pornography: A national survey of police officers and staff in England and Wales', *Journal of Interpersonal Violence*, https://journals.sagepub.com/doi/10.1177/0886260518760011

Boulos, Janay. (2019) 'Cyber flashing: "I froze when penis picture dropped on to my phone"', *BBC News*, 26 April, www.bbc.co.uk/news/uk-48054893

Branigin, Anne. (2016) 'Some pervert cyberflashed on the subway – And I have my iPhone to thank', *Splinter News*, 29 November, https://splinternews.com/some-pervert-cyberflashed-me-on-the-subway-and-i-have-m-1793864020

Brison, Susan. (2003) 'Beauvoir and feminism: Interview and reflections', in Claudia Card (ed) *The Cambridge Companion to Simone de Beauvoir*, Cambridge: Cambridge University Press, pp 189–207.

Brooks-Hay, Oona. (2020) 'Doing the "right thing"? Understanding why rape victim-survivors report to the police', *Feminist Criminology*, 15(2): 174–195.

Brunt, Martin. (2020) 'Coronavirus: BAME groups disproportionately fined for COVID-19 breaches', *Sky News*, 27 July, https://news.sky.com/story/coronavirus-bame-groups-disproportionately-fined-for-covid-19-breaches-12037297

Bumiller, Kristin. (2008) *In an Abusive State: How Neoliberalism Appropriated the Feminist Movement against Sexual Violence*, Durham, NC: Duke University Press.

Burgess, Matt (2020) 'Deepfake porn is now mainstream. And major sites are cashing in', *Wired*, 27 August, www.wired.co.uk/article/deepfake-porn-websites-videos-law

Burgin, Rachael. (2018) 'Persistent narratives of force and resistance: Affirmative consent as law reform', *British Journal of Criminology*, 59(2): 296–314.

Burkett, Melissa. (2015) 'Sex(t) talk: A qualitative analysis of young adults' negotiations of the pleasures and perils of sexting', *Sexuality and Culture*, 19(4): 835–863.

Candeub, Adam. (1994) 'Motive crimes and other minds', *University of Pennsylvania Law Review*, 142: 2071–2123.

Chalmers, James and Leverick, Fiona. (2017) *The Criminal Law of Scotland*, Vol 2 (4th edn), Edinburgh: Green.

Chesney, Bobby and Citron, Danielle Keats. (2019) 'Deep fakes: A looming challenge for privacy, democracy and national security', *California Law Review*, 107: 1753–1820.

Choudhry, Shazia. (2016) 'Towards a transformative conceptualisation of violence against women: A critical frame analysis of Council of Europe discourse on violence against women', *Modern Law Review*, 79(3): 406–441.

Citizens' Voice. (2019) 'Proceed with plan against cyberflashing', 30 September, www.citizensvoice.com/opinion/proceed-with-plan-against-cyber-flashing-1.2539616

Citron, Danielle Keats. (2010) 'Civil rights in our information age', in Saul Levmore and Martha Nussbaum (eds) *The Offensive Internet*, Cambridge, MA: Harvard University Press.

Citron, Danielle Keats. (2014) *Hate Crimes in Cyber Space*, Cambridge, MA: Harvard University Press.

Citron, Danielle Keats. (2015) 'Addressing cyber-harassment: An overview of hate crimes in cyberspace', *Journal of Law, Technology and the Internet*, 6: 1–12.

Citron, Danielle Keats. (2019) 'Sexual privacy', *Yale Law Journal*, 128: 1874–1960.

City Council of New York. (2019) 'Transcript of minutes of Public Safety Committee', 27 June.

Closson, Troy. (2019) 'A new Texas law criminalizes sending unwanted nudes. Lawyers say it might be difficult to enforce', *Texas Tribune*, 14 August, www.texastribune.org/2019/08/14/Texas-new-law-sending-unwanted-nudes-dating-apps-texts/

Coble, Sarah. (2019) 'Pennsylvania might be second state to criminalise cyber flashing', *Infosecurity*, 30 September, www.infosecurity-magazine.com/news/pennsylvania-might-criminalize/

Collins, Patricia Hill. (1997) 'Comment on Hekman's "Truth and Method: Feminist Standpoint Theory Revisited": Where's the power?', *Signs*, 22: 375–381.

Collins, Patricia Hill. (2000) 'Gender, black feminism, and black political economy', *Annals of the American Academy of Political and Social Science*, 568(1): 41–53.

Conaghan, Joanne. (1996) 'Gendered harms and the law of tort: Remedying (sexual) harassment', *Oxford Journal of Legal Studies*, 16(3): 407–431.

Conaghan, Joanne. (2013) *Law and Gender*, Oxford: Oxford University Press.

Crenshaw, Kimberle. (1991) 'Mapping the margins: Intersectionality, identity politics, and violence against women of color', *Stanford Law Review*, 43(6): 1241–1299.

Crocker, Diane. (2008) 'Criminalizing harassment and the transformative potential of law', *Canadian Journal of Women and the Law*, 20(1): 87–110.

Crofts, Thomas and Kirchengast, Tyrone. (2019) 'A ladder approach to criminalising revenge pornography', *Journal of Criminal Law*, 83(1): 87–103.

Crown Prosecution Service. (2018) 'Stalking and harassment', 23 May, www.cps.gov.uk/legal-guidance/stalking-and-harassment

Crown Prosecution Service. (2020) 'Rape and sexual offences: Chapter 2', www.cps.gov.uk/legal-guidance/rape-and-sexual-offences-chapter-2-sexual-offences-act-2003-principal-offences-and

Dahl, Stang. (1987) *Women's Law: An Introduction to Feminist Jurisprudence*, New York: Oxford University Press.

Daily Mail. (2014) 'Builder ordered to pay policeman £400 after drawing two penises on picture of him and posting it to Facebook', 5 February, www.dailymail.co.uk/news/article-2552269/Builder-ordered-pay-policeman-400-drawing-two-penises-picture-posting-Facebook.html

Daly, Kathleen. (2014) 'Reconceptualizing sexual victimization and justice', in Inge Vanfraechem, Anthony Pemberton and Felix Mukwiza Ndahinda (eds) *Perspectives on Rights, Transition and Reconciliation*, Oxford: Routledge, pp 378–395.

Dawson, Brit. (2019) 'Is an unsolicited dick pic ban progressive or just lame?', *Dazed*, 23 September, www.dazeddigital.com/life-culture/article/46122/1/texas-unsolicited-dick-pic-ban-progressive-or-lame-bumble-grindr-lgbtq

Day, Aviah and Gill, Aisha. (2020) 'Applying intersectionality to partnerships between women's organizations and the criminal justice system in relation to domestic violence', *British Journal of Criminology*, 60(4): 830–850.

Dean, James. (2015) 'Cyber flasher sends lewd image to woman's phone', *The Times*, 14 August, www.thetimes.co.uk/article/cyber-flasher-sends-lewd-image-to-womans-phone-t0b00lw2dp9

Dixon, Ejeris and Lakshmi Piepzna-Samarasinha, Leah. (2020) *Beyond Survival: Strategies and Stories from the Transformative Justice Movement*, Chico, CA: AK Press.

Eaton, Asia and McGlynn, Clare. (2020) 'The psychology of nonconsensual porn: Understanding and addressing a growing form of sexual violence', *Policy Insights from the Behavioral and Brain Sciences*, 7(2): 190–197.

Eterovic-Soric, Brett, Kim-Kwang, Raymond, Ashman, Helen and Mubarak, Sameera. (2017) 'Stalking the stalkers – detecting and deterring stalking behaviours using technology: A review', *Computers and Security*, 70: 278–289.

European Parliament. (2018) 'Cyber violence and hate speech online against women', Policy Department for Citizens' Rights and Constitutional Affairs, September, PE 604.979, www.europarl.europa.eu/RegData/etudes/STUD/2018/604979/IPOL_STU(2018)604979_EN.pdf

Fairbrother, Nichole and Rachman, Stanley. (2004) 'Feelings of mental pollution subsequent to sexual assault', *Behaviour Research and Therapy*, 42(2): 173–189.

Fight the New Drug. (2019) 'Digital exhibitionism: Why strangers are AirDropping nudes to unsuspecting recipients', 27 June, https://fightthenewdrug.org/digital-exhibitionism-strangers-are-now-airdropping-nudes-to-unsuspecting-recipients/

Fileborn, Bianca. (2017) 'Justice 2.0: Street harassment victims' use of social media and online activism as sites of informal justice', *British Journal of Criminology*, 57(6): 1482–1501.

Fileborn, Bianca and Vera-Gray, Fiona. (2017) '"I want to be able to walk the street without fear": Transforming justice for street harassment', *Feminist Legal Studies*, 25: 203–227.

Fitzgerald, Frances. (2016) Seanad Eireann debate, Criminal Law (Sexual Offences) Bill 2015 (Committee Stage), 245(2), 14 January, www.oireachtas.ie/en/debates/debate/seanad/2016-01-14/12/

Franks, Mary Ann. (2012) 'Sexual harassment 2.0', *Maryland Law Review*, 71(3): 55–704.

Franks, Mary Ann. (2017) 'Redefining "revenge porn" reform: A view from the front lines', *Florida Law Review*, 69(5): 1251–1337.

Fraser, Nancy. (2012) 'Feminism, capitalism, and the cunning of history', *HAL*, 2–4.

Fricker, Miranda. (2007) *Epistemic Injustice: Power and the Ethics of Knowing*, Oxford: Oxford University Press.

Fulu, Emma, Warner, Xian, Miedema, Stephanie, Jewkes, Rachel, Roselli, Tim and Lang, James. (2013) 'Why do some men use violence against women and how can we prevent it?' *Partners for Prevention*, www.partners4prevention.org/sites/default/files/resources/p4p-report.pdf.

Gallagher, Sophie. (2017) 'How smartphones and technology are "ushering in a new wave of sex offenders"', *Huffington Post*, 27 August, www.huffingtonpost.co.uk/entry/digital-age-ushered-in-new-wave-of-sex-offenders-who-would-not-previously-have-committed-crimes-says-expert_uk_599fd8a5e4b0821444c26eb1

Gallagher, Sophie. (2018a) '9 women tell us why the UK needs a cyber flashing law: "We need to feel safe in public"', *Huffington Post*, 20 November, www.huffingtonpost.co.uk/entry/why-the-uk-needs-a-cyberflashing-law_uk_5bed94c1e4b0dbb7ea6852fc

Gallagher, Sophie. (2018b) 'Cyber flashing and flashing can be equally harmful, says woman who experienced both', *Huffington Post*, 4 December, www.huffingtonpost.co.uk/entry/cyberflashing-real-life-vs-flashing-online_uk_5bfe81ede4b030172fa8d278

Gallagher, Sophie. (2018c) 'Cyber flashing: Why are men still sending women unsolicited dick pics?', *Huffington Post*, 6 November, www.huffingtonpost.co.uk/entry/cyberflashing-why-are-men-still-sending-women-unsolicited-dick-pics_uk_5bdc278fe4b04367a87b755e

Gallagher, Sophie. (2018d) '"Unacceptable": Women cyber flashed on British Airways flight criticise airline response', *Huffington Post*, 12 November, www.huffingtonpost.co.uk/entry/women-cyberflashed-on-british-airways-flight-say-airlines-response-is-completely-unacceptable_uk_5be598f5e4b0dbe871aa2d73

Gallagher, Sophie. (2018e) '"Violated, sick, uncomfortable": 10 women on being sent unsolicited dick pics', *Huffington Post*, 26 October, www.huffingtonpost.co.uk/entry/it-was-scary-not-knowing-who-might-follow-me-off-the-train-women-talk-about-how-it-feels-to-be-sent-unsolicited-dick-pics_uk_5bcec723e4b0d38b587baa52

Gallagher, Sophie. (2018f) 'Would you rename your phone to avoid unsolicited dick pics? This woman did', *Huffington Post*, 30 October, www.huffingtonpost.co.uk/entry/it-has-become-second-nature-to-protect-myself-these-women-are-changing-their-behaviour-to-avoid-becoming-victims-of-cyberflashing_uk_5bd6d0f8e4b0a8f17ef9778a

Gallagher, Sophie. (2019a) 'Cyber flashing: 70 women on what it's like to be sent unsolicited dick pics', *Huffington Post*, 21 May, www.huffingtonpost.co.uk/entry/cyberflashing-70-women-on-what-its-like-to-be-sent-unsolicited-dick-pics_uk_5cd59005e4b0705e47db0195

Gallagher, Sophie. (2019b) 'Cyber flashing arrests rise but still no prosecutions, as victims wait for law review', *Huffington Post*, 14 August, www.huffingtonpost.co.uk/entry/cyber-flashing-arrests-rise-but-still-no-prosecutions-as-victims-wait-for-law-review_uk_5d53c556e4b0c63bcbefaa10

Gallagher, Sophie. (2019c) 'Cyber flashing: Facebook Messenger will now protect under 18s from strangers', *Huffington Post*, 26 April, www.huffingtonpost.co.uk/entry/cyberflashing-facebook-messenger-will-now-protect-under-18s-from-strangers_uk_5c65755ae4b0bcddd40f40f9

Gallagher, Sophie. (2019d) 'Cyber flashing: I had to educate police about the crime I was trying to report', *Huffington Post*, 16 May, www.huffingtonpost.co.uk/entry/woman-has-to-educate-police-after-being-cyberflashed-it-shouldnt-be-victims-job-to-explain-the-tech_uk_5cd156e7e4b0548b735f85a6

Gallagher, Sophie. (2019e) 'Cyber flashing victims on the moment they realised they weren't alone', *Huffington Post*, 12 July, www.huffingtonpost.co.uk/entry/would-making-cyberflashing-illegal-stop-people-sending-dick-pics_uk_5c50674fe4b0d9f9be6951ce

Gallagher, Sophie. (2019f) '"He was staring at me across the concourse, his hands were shaking": Why cyber flashing isn't just a digital problem', *Huffington Post*, 2 May, www.huffingtonpost.co.uk/entry/he-was-staring-at-me-across-the-concourse-his-hands-were-shaking-why-cyberflashing-isnt-just-a-digital-problem_uk_5ca1ca0de4b0bc0dacab0dd0

Gallagher, Sophie. (2019g) 'The worrying rise of the Facebook flasher – And what the site is doing about it', *Huffington Post*, 20 February, www.huffingtonpost.co.uk/entry/rise-of-the-facebook-flasher-messenger_uk_5c6308b7e4b0b50014aa716a

Gallagher, Sophie. (2019h) 'Would making cyberflashing illegal stop people sending dick pics', *Huffington Post*, 10 June, www.huffingtonpost.co.uk/entry/would-making-cyberflashing-illegal-stop-people-sending-dick-pics_uk_5c50674fe4b0d9f9be6951ce

Gallagher, Sophie. (2020) '"The tip of the iceberg": Cyber-flashing on trains "largely unreported" despite huge rise in incidents', *The Independent*, 18 February, www.independent.co.uk/life-style/women/cyber-flashing-incidents-number-2020-a9341676.html

Gamez-Gaudix, Manuel, Almendros, Carmen, Borrajo, Erika and Calvete, Esther. (2015) 'Prevalence and association of sexting and online sexual victimization among Spanish adults', *Sexuality Research and Social Policy*, 12: 145–154.

Gavey, Nicola and Schmidt, Johanna. (2011) '"Trauma of rape" discourse: A double-edged template for everyday understandings of the impact of rape?', *Violence Against Women*, 17(4): 433–456.

Gekoski, Anna, Gray, Jacqueline, Horvarth, Miranda, Edwards, Sarah, Emirali, Aliye and Adler, Joanna. (2015) *What Works in Reducing Sexual Harassment and Sexual Offences on Public Transport Nationally and Internationally*, London: British Transport Police and Department for Transport.

Gil, Natalie. (2019) 'Women who've been cyberflashed on why dick pics are no laughing matter', *Refinery29*, 8 February, www.refinery29.com/en-gb/2019/01/222278/cyberflashing-dick-pics

Giladi, Paul. (2018) 'Epistemic injustice: A role for recognition', *Philosophy and Social Criticism*, 44(2): 141–158.

Gillespie, Alisdair. (2019) 'Tackling voyeurism: Is the Voyeurism (Offences) Act 2019 a wasted opportunity?', *Modern Law Review*, 82: 1107–1131.

Gillett, Rosalie. (2018) 'Intimate intrusions online: Studying the normalization of abuse in dating apps', *Women's Studies International Forum*, 69: 212–219.

Gizauskas, Rosie. (2018) 'Anti-social media: From WhatsApp to dating apps, Fabulous investigates the cyber flashers invading your inbox and why d★★k pics have gone next-level', *The Sun*, 16 December, www.thesun.co.uk/fabulous/7966974/cyber-flashers-invading-your-inbox/

Glitch UK. (2020) 'Impact of online abuse', https://fixtheglitch.org/impactofonlineabuse/

Glitch UK and EVAW. (2020) 'The ripple effect: COVID-19 and the epidemic of online abuse', September, www.endviolenceagainstwomen.org.uk/wp-content/uploads/Glitch-and-EVAW-The-Ripple-Effect-Online-abuse-during-COVID-19-Sept-2020.pdf

Gollayan, Christian. (2018) 'NYC women: Stop sending us penis pics!', *New York Post*, 8 August, https://nypost.com/2018/08/08/nyc-women-stop-sending-us-penis-pics/

Goodmark, Leigh. (2018) *Decriminalising Domestic Violence*, Berkley, CA: University of California Press.

Gore, Ashlee. (2020) 'It's all or nothing: Consent, reasonable belief, and the continuum of sexual violence in judicial logic', *Social and Legal Studies*, https://journals.sagepub.com/doi/abs/10.1177/0964663920947813

Gotell, Lise. (2015) 'Reassessing the place of criminal law reform in the struggle against sexual violence', in Anastasia Powell, Nicola Henry and Asher Flynn (eds) *Rape Justice*, London: Palgrave Macmillan, pp 53–71.

Gray, Jacqueline. (2015) 'What constitutes a "reasonable belief" in consent to sex? A thematic analysis', *Journal of Sexual Aggression*, 21(3): 337–353.

Graycar, Regina and Morgan, Jenny. (2002) *The Hidden Gender of Law* (2nd edn), Sydney: Federation Press.

Green, Stuart. (2018) 'To see and be seen: Reconstructing the law of voyeurism and exhibitionism', *American Criminal Law Review*, 55: 203–258.

Gruber, Aya. (2020) *The Feminist War on Crime*, Berkeley, CA: University of California Press.

Hall, Matthew and Hearn, Jeff. (2017) *Revenge Pornography*, London: Routledge.

Hanmer, Jalna and Saunders, Sheila. (1984) *Well-Founded Fear*, London: Hutchinson.

Harris, Bridget and Vitis, Laura. (2020) 'Digital intrusions: Technology, spatiality and violence against women', *Journal of Gender Based Violence*, 4(3): 325–341.

Hayes, Rebecca and Dragiewicz, Molly. (2018) 'Unsolicited dick pics: Erotica, exhibitionism or entitlement?', *Women's Studies International Forum*, 71: 114–120.

Henry, Nicola and Powell, Anastasia. (2015) 'Embodied harms', *Violence Against Women*, 21(6): 758–779.

Henry, Nicola and Powell, Anastasia. (2016) 'Technology-facilitated sexual violence: A literature review of empirical research', *Trauma, Violence and Abuse*, 19(2): 195–208.

Henry, Nicola, McGlynn, Clare, Flynn, Asher, Johnson, Kelly, Powell, Anastasia and Scott, Adrian. (2020) *Image-Based Sexual Abuse: A Study on the Causes and Consequences of Non-Consensual Nude or Sexual Imagery*, London: Routledge.

Herman, Judith. (2005) 'Justice from the victim's perspective', *Violence Against Women*, 11(5): 571–602.

Hohl, Katrin and Stanko, Elisabeth. (2015) 'Complaints of rape and the criminal justice system: Fresh evidence on the attrition problem in England and Wales', *European Journal of Criminology*, 12(3): 324–341.

Holder, Robyn. (2015) 'Satisfied? Exploring victims' justice judgments', in Dean Wilson and Ross Stuart (eds) *Crime, Victims and Police*, Basingstoke: Palgrave Macmillan, pp. 184–213.

Holmes, Alex. (2019) 'Bumble to launch software that blurs dick pics and graphic images', *Metro News*, 25 April, https://metro.co.uk/2019/04/25/bumble-to-launch-dick-pic-detector-to-end-reign-of-unsolicited-pics-9316489/

Home Office. (2000) *Setting the Boundaries: Reforming the Law on Sexual Offences*, London: Home Office.

Home Office. (2002) *Protecting the Public: Strengthening Protection against Sex Offenders and Reforming the Law on Sexual Offences*, Cm 5668, London: Home Office.

Hopewell, Luke. (2014) 'Australian man jailed for unsolicited sexting', *Gizmodo*, 12 September, www.gizmodo.com.au/2014/09/australian-man-jailed-for-unsolicited-sexting/

Husak, Douglas. (2008) *Overcriminalization*, New York: Oxford University Press.

Hussain, Saddham. (2019) 'Prospective amendments to Singapore's penal code', *Court Uncourt*, 6(1): 44–47.

Imkaan and EVAW. (2016) 'Powerful new film: Black women speak out about racist sexual harassment', www.endviolenceagainstwomen.org.uk/powerful-new-film-black-women-speak-out-about-racist-sexual-harassment/

Irish Legal News. (2018) 'Forensics expert moots penile database to tackle sex crime', 3 September, https://irishlegal.com/article/forensics-expert-moots-penile-database-to-tackle-sex-crime

Johansen, Katrine and Tjornhoj-Thomsen, Tine. (nd) '"It's like you're almost being exposed to like a flasher": Unwanted digital sexual attention and gendered vulnerability in a Nordic context', *Justis Ministeriet*, www.justitsministeriet.dk/sites/default/files/media/Arbejdsomraader/Forskning/Forskningspuljen/2019/artikel_til_jm_-_katrine_bindesboel_holm_johansen.pdf

Johnson, Ian. (2018) 'Women want men who send pictures of their genitals to be classed as sex offenders', *Chronicle Live*, 17 June, www.chroniclelive.co.uk/news/north-east-news/women-want-men-who-send-14753379

Kahan, Dan. (2000) 'Gentle nudges vs hard shoves: solving the sticky norms problem', *University of Chicago Law Review*, 67(3): 607–645.

Kelly, Liz. (1988) *Surviving Sexual Violence*, Cambridge: Polity.

Kelly, Liz. (2003) 'The wrong debate: Reflections on why force is not the key issue with respect to trafficking in women for sexual exploitation', *Feminist Review*, 73(1): 139–144.

Kelly, Liz, Burton, Sheila and Regan, Linda. (1996) 'Beyond victim or survivor: Sexual violence, identity and feminist theory and practice', in Lisa Adkins and Vicki Merchant (eds) *Sexualizing the Social*, New York: St Martin's Press, pp 77–101.

Kim, Mimi. (2018) 'From carceral feminism to transformative justice: Women-of-color feminism and alternatives to incarceration', *Journal of Ethnic and Cultural Diversity in Social Work*, 27(3): 219–233.

Kurzius, Rachel. (2019) 'Someone AirDropped a woman an unsolicited dick pic during her metro commute', *Dcist*, 11 March, https://dcist.com/story/19/03/11/someone-airdropped-a-woman-an-unsolicited-dick-pic-during-her-metro-commute/

Kwang, Kevin. (2019) 'Voyeurism, "cyber flashing": Emerging new crimes targeted under Criminal Law Reform Bill', *CNA*, 11 February, www.channelnewsasia.com/news/singapore/voyeurism-cyber-flashing-emerging-new-crimes-targeted-under-11229142?cid=h3_referral_inarticlelinks_24082018_cna

Lacey, Nicola. (2009) 'Historicising criminalisation: Conceptual and empirical issues', *Modern Law Review*, 72(6): 936–60.

Lacey, Nicola and Hannah Pickard. (2015) 'To blame or to forgive? Reconciling punishment and forgiveness in criminal justice', *Oxford Journal of Legal Studies*, 35(4): 665–696.

Langlois, Ganaele and Slane, Andrea. (2017) 'Economies of reputation: The case of revenge porn', *Communications and Critical/Cultural Studies*, 14(2): 120–138.

Larcombe, Wendy, Fileborn, Biance, Powell, Anastasia, Hanley, Natalia and Henry, Nicola. (2016) '"I think it's rape and I think he would be found not guilty": Focus group perceptions of (un)reasonable belief in consent in rape law', *Social and Legal Studies*, 25(5): 611–629.

Law Commission. (2015) *Simplification of Criminal Law: Public Nuisance and Outraging Public Decency*, London: Law Commission.

Law Commission. (2018) *Abusive and Offensive Online Communications: A Scoping Report*, London: Law Commission.

Law Commission. (2020) *Harmful Online Communications: The Criminal Offence*, London: Law Commission.

Law Reform Commission of Hong Kong. (2012) *Review of Sexual Offences*, Hong Kong: Law Reform Commission.

Lee, Yung-Mi. (2019) 'Testimony of Young-Mi Lee, Brooklyn Defender Services', 27 June, https://legistar. council.nyc.gov/View.ashx?M=F&ID=7538639&GUI D=2DA9779D-FAD3-4989-A5C1-A1F30DF9B325

Lees, Paris. (2015) 'Mya Taylor on being a trans actor, race, gender and intersectionality', *The Independent*, 7 November, www.independent.co.uk/arts-entertainment/music/features/mya-taylor-being-trans-actor-race-gender-and-intersectionality-a6724321. html

Levya, Connie. (2020) 'Senator Leyva introduces FLASH Act to ban sending unsolicited lewd pictures and video', 20 February, https:// sd20.senate.ca.gov/news/2020-02-20-senator-leyva-introduces-flash-act-ban-sending-unsolicited-lewd-pictures-and-videos

Ley, David. (2016) 'Why men send pics of their junk', *Psychology Today*, 18 February, www.psychologytoday.com/us/blog/women-who-stray/201602/why-men-send-pics-their-junk

Light, Ben. (2016) 'Producing sexual cultures and pseudonymous publics with digital networks', in Rebecca Lind (ed) *Race and Gender in Electronic Media*, New York: Routledge.

Lih Yi, Beh (2019) '"Pervasive" digital sexual violence against women skyrockets in Singapore', *Thomson Reuters Foundation*, 25 November, www.reuters.com/article/us-singapore-crime-technology-women/pervasive-digital-sexual-violence-against-women-skyrockets-in-singapore-idUSKBN1XZ1NB

Livingstone, Tom. (2018) 'School kids putting themselves at risk "pranking" strangers with AirDrop porn', 14 May, *News.com.au*, www.news.com.au/technology/school-kids-putting-themselves-at-risk-pranking-strangers-with-airdrop-porn/news-story/8f65a97dbb9bc70709a18a6b64ee5320

Lonsway, Kimberley and Archambault, Joanne. (2012) 'The "justice gap" for sexual assault cases: Future directions for research and reform', *Violence Against Women*, 18(2): 145–168.

Lumsden, Karen and Harmer, Emily. (2019) *Online Othering*, Basingstoke: Palgrave Macmillan.

Lundgren, Eva. (1998) 'The hand that strikes and comforts: Gender construction and the tension between body and soul', in Emerson Dobash and Russell Dobash (eds) *Rethinking Violence Against Women*, Thousand Oaks, CA: Sage, pp 169–196.

Mackay, Irene and Earnshaw, Jill. (1995) 'Skirting around sexual harassment', *New Law Journal*, 145(6686): 145–338.

MacKinnon, Catharine. (1979) *Sexual Harassment of Working Women*, New Haven, CT: Yale University Press.

MacKinnon, Catharine. (2017) *Butterfly Politics*, Cambridge, MA: Harvard University Press.

Mair, George. (2018) 'Top Scottish forensic expert Professor Dame Sue Black calls for cops to create sex offender's PENIS database to snare paedos', *The Sun*, 2 September, www.thescottishsun.co.uk/news/3150836/forensics-privates-sue-black-database/

Mandau, Morten. (2020) '"Directly in your face": A qualitative study on the sending and receiving of unsolicited "dick pics" among young adults', *Sexuality and Culture*, 24(1): 72–93.

Mann, Ruth and Hollin, Clive. (2007) 'Sexual offenders' explanations for their offending', *Journal of Sexual Aggression*, 13(1): 3–9.

March, Evita and Wagstaff, Danielle. (2017) 'Sending nudes: Sex, self-rated mate value, and trait Machiavellianism predict sending unsolicited explicit images', *Frontiers in Psychology*, 18 December, www.frontiersin.org/articles/10.3389/fpsyg.2017.02210/full

Marcotte, Alexandra, Gesselman, Amanda, Fisher, Helen and Garcia, Justin. (2020) 'Women's and men's reactions to receiving unsolicited genital images from men', *Journal of Sex Research*, www.tandfonline.com/doi/abs/10.1080/00224499.2020.1779171

Masson, Amy. (2020) 'A critique of anti-carceral feminism', *Journal of International Women's Studies*, 21(3): 64–76.

McGlynn, Clare. (2017) 'Watching porn in public: A modern form of street harassment?', *Huffington Post*, 19 January, www.huffingtonpost.co.uk/clare-mcglynn/watching-porn-in-public-a_2_b_14268708.html

McGlynn, Clare. (2018) '"Revenge porn"' and upskirting remind us sexual offending is not about sexual arousal', *Huffington Post*, 11 July, www.huffingtonpost.co.uk/entry/revenge-porn-and-why-sexual-offending-is-not-about_uk_5b45c9e7e4b00db1492ffe9f

McGlynn, Clare. (2019) 'Cyber flashing and deepfake porn are harming women right now – They need more urgent protection', *Huffington Post*, 26 June, www.huffingtonpost.co.uk/entry/cyberflashing-revenge-porn_uk_5d135cc0e4b0aa375f569133

McGlynn, Clare and Johnson, Kelly. (2020) 'Submission to Law Commission consultation on harmful online communications offences', 18 December, https://claremcglynn.com/cyberflashing/

McGlynn, Clare and Rackley, Erika. (2009) 'Criminalising extreme pornography: A lost opportunity', *Criminal Law Review*, 4: 245–260.

McGlynn, Clare and Rackley, Erika. (2017) 'Image-based sexual abuse', *Oxford Journal of Legal Studies*, 37(3): 534–561.

McGlynn, Clare and Vera-Gray, Fiona. (2018) 'No woman in a public place is free from the risk of upskirting – We must do more to tackle image-based sexual abuse', *Huffington Post*, 23 November, www.huffingtonpost.co.uk/entry/upskirting-law-sexual-harassment_uk_5bf7c501e4b088e1a6888e47

McGlynn, Clare and Vera-Gray, Fiona. (2019) 'Porn website T&Cs are a work of fiction. We need radical measures to take them on', *Huffington Post*, 28 June, www.huffingtonpost.co.uk/entry/porn-website-tcs_uk_5d132febe4b09125ca466358

McGlynn, Clare and Westmarland, Nicole. (2019) 'Kaleidoscopic justice: Sexual violence and victim-survivors' perceptions of justice', *Social and Legal Studies*, 28(2): 179–201.

McGlynn, Clare, Westmarland, Nicole and Godden, Nikki. (2012) '"I just wanted him to hear me": Sexual violence and the possibilities of restorative justice', *Journal of Law and Society*, 39(2): 213–240.

McGlynn, Clare, Rackley, Erika and Houghton, Ruth. (2017) 'Beyond "revenge porn": The continuum of image-based sexual abuse', *Feminist Legal Studies*, 25(1): 25–46.

McGlynn, Clare, Rackley, Erika, Johnson, Kelly, Henry, Nicola, Flynn, Asher, Powell, Anastasia, Gavey, Nicola and Scott, Adrian. (2019) 'Shattering lives and myths: A report on image-based sexual abuse', https://dro.dur.ac.uk/28683/3/28683.pdf?DDD34+DDD19+

McGlynn, Clare, Johnson, Kelly, Rackley, Erika, Henry, Nicola, Gavey, Nicola, Flynn, Asher and Powell, Anastasia. (2020) '"It's torture for the soul": The harms of image-based sexual abuse', *Social and Legal Studies*, https://journals.sagepub.com/doi/full/10.1177/0964663920947791

McKeever, Natasha. (2019) 'Can a woman rape a man and why does it matter?', *Criminal Law Philosophy*, 13: 599–619.

McNeill, Sandra. (1987) 'Flashing – Its effect on women', in Jalna Hanmer and Mary Maynard (eds) *Women, Violence and Social Control*, Basingstoke: Macmillan.

Meineck, Sebastian. (2020) '"Zoom bombers" are still blasting private meetings with disturbing and graphic content', *Vice*, 10 June, www.vice.com/en/article/m7je5y/zoom-bombers-private-calls-disturbing-content

Miller, James. (2014) 'The fourth screen: Mediatization and the smartphone', *Mobile Media and Communication*, 2(2): 209–226.

Ministry of Law. (2018) 'Public consultation on proposed amendments to the penal code', 9 September, www.reach.gov.sg/participate/public-consultation/ministry-of-home-affairs/public-consultation-on-proposed-amendments-to-the-penal-code

Munro, Vanessa. (2007) *Law and Politics at the Perimeter*, Oxford: Hart.

Naffine, Ngaire. (1990) *Law and the Sexes*, London: Allen and Unwin.

Narayan, V. (2019) 'Mumbai: Man makes video call to scriptwriter and flashes her', *Times of India*, 14 July.

Norrie, Alan. (2005) *Law and the Beautiful Soul*, London: Glasshouse Publishing.

North Yorkshire Police Fire and Crime Commissioner. (2018) 'No more naming', www.northyorkshire-pfcc.gov.uk/content/uploads/2018/11/Suffering-in-Silence-Report.pdf

O'Malley, Tom. (2017) 'Criminal Law (Sexual Offences) Act 2017: The offence provisions', www.dppireland.ie/app/uploads/2017/11/PAPER_-_Tom_OMalley_BL.1.pdf

Ormerod, David and Laird, Karl. (2018) *Smith, Hogan and Ormerod's Criminal Law* (15th edn), Oxford: Oxford University Press.

Oswald, Flora, Lopes, Alex, Skoda, Kaylee, Hesse, Cassandra and Pedersen, Cory. (2020) 'I'll show you mine so you'll show me yours: Motivations and personality variables in photographic exhibitionism', *Journal of Sex Research*, 57(5): 597–609.

Otterman, Sharon. (2020) 'Sending lewd nudes to strangers could mean a year in jail', *New York Times*, 30 November, www.nytimes.com/2018/11/30/nyregion/airdrop-sexual-harassment.html

Paasonen, Susanna, Light, Ben and Jarrett, Kylie. (2019) 'The dick pic: Harassment, curation, and desire', *Social Media + Society*, 2: 1–10.

Pain, Rachel. (1993) 'Women's fear of sexual violence: Explaining the spatial paradox', in Huw Jones (ed) *Crime and the Environment*, Aldershot: Avebury.

Palermino, Charlotte. (2018) 'The AirDropped dick pic epidemic is upon us', *Elle*, 21 March, www.elle.com/culture/tech/a19549140/the-airdropped-dickpic-epidemic-is-upon-us/

Park, Chang Sup and Kaye, Barbara. (2018) 'Smartphone and self-extension: Functionally, anthropomorphically, and onto-logically extending self via the smartphone', *Mobile Media and Communication*, 7(2): 215–231.

PCRP. (2018) *Penal Code Review Committee Report*, August, www.reach.gov.sg/-/media/reach/old-reach/2018/public-consult/mha/annex–pcrc-report.ashx

Perry, Tod. (2019) 'NSFW: A student collected over 300 d★★k pics on Tinder and turned them into an art project', *Good*, 26 July, www.good.is/articles/d-pics-art-project

Pew Research Centre. (2017) 'Online harassment 2017', 11 July, www.pewresearch.org/internet/2017/07/11/online-harassment-2017/

Porter, Antonia. (2020) *Prosecuting Domestic Abuse in Neoliberal Times: Amplifying the Survivor's Voice*, Basingstoke: Palgrave.

Powell, Anastasia and Henry, Nicola. (2017) *Sexual Violence in a Digital Age*, Basingstoke: Palgrave Macmillan.

Precel, Nicole. (2019) 'Ursula didn't know what cyber flashing was until the day at the museum', *Sydney Morning Herald*, 20 June, www.smh.com.au/national/ursula-didn-t-know-what-cyber-flashing-was-until-the-day-at-the-museum-20190512-p51mm6.html

Prison Reform Trust. (2019) *Prison: The Facts*, London: Prison Reform Trust.

Reaume, Denise. (2003) 'Discrimination and dignity', *Louisiana Law Review*, 63(3): 645–695.

Ricciardelli, Rosemary and Adorjan, Michael. (2019) '"If a girl's photo gets sent around, that's a way bigger deal than if a guy's photo gets sent around": Gender, sexting, and the teenage years', *Journal of Gender Studies*, 28(5): 563–577.

Richardson, Ingrid. (2012) 'Touching the screen: A phenomenology of mobile gaming and the iPhone', in Larrisa Hjorth, Jean Burgess and Ingrid Richardson (eds) *Studying Mobile Media*, New York: Routledge, pp 133–154.

Ringrose, Jessica. (2020) 'Is there hidden sexual abuse going on in your school?', *TES*, 29 October, www.tes.com/news/there-hidden-sexual-abuse-going-your-school

Ringrose, Jessica and Lawrence, Emily. (2018) 'Remixing misandry, manspreading, and dick pics: Networked feminist humour on Tumblr', *Feminist Media Studies*, 18(2): 1–19.

Riordan, Sharon. (1999) 'Indecent exposure: The impact upon the victim's fear of sexual crime', *Journal of Forensic Psychiatry*, 10(2): 309–316.

Roach, April. (2020) 'Pick-up artist known as "Addy A-game" has conviction for targeting women quashed on appeal', *Standard*, 18 September, www.standard.co.uk/news/crime/glasgow-pick-up-artist-conviction-quashed-a4551016.html

Robertiello, Gina and Terry, Karen. (2007) 'Can we profile sex offenders? A review of sex offender typologies', *Aggression and Violent Behaviour*, 12(5): 508–518.

Robinson, Ben and Dowling, Nicola. (2019) 'Revenge porn laws "not working", says victims group', *BBC News*, 18 May, www.bbc.co.uk/news/uk-48309752

Robson, John (ed). (1977) *Collected Works of John Stuart Mill, Essays on Politics and Society*, Vol 18, London: Routledge.

Rogers, Stephen. (2016) 'Facebook images of young Cork girls posted on porn site', *Irish Examiner*, 14 January, www.irishexaminer.com/ireland/facebook-images-of-young-cork-girls-posted-on-porn-site-376096.html

Rook, Peter and Ward, Robert. (2016) *Sexual Offences Law and Practice* (5th edn), London: Sweet and Maxwell.

Salter, Michael. (2016) 'Privates in the online public: Sex(ting) and reputation on social media', *New Media and Society*, 18(11): 2723–2739.

Sarner, Moya. (2019) 'What makes men send dick pics?', *The Guardian*, 8 January, www.theguardian.com/society/2019/jan/08/what-makes-men-send-dick-pics

School of Sexuality Education. (2020) 'Policies and guidance', https://schoolofsexed.org/guidance-for-schools

Scottish Law Commission. (2006) *Discussion Paper on Rape and Other Sexual Offences*, Edinburgh: Scottish Law Commission.

Scottish Law Commission. (2007) *Report on Rape and Other Sexual Offences*, Edinburgh: Scottish Law Commission.

Scully, Diana and Marolla, Joseph. (1985) '"Riding the bull at the Gilley's": Convicted rapists describe the rewards of rape', in Claire Renzetti and Raquel Kennedy Bergen (eds) *Violence Against Women: Classic Papers*, Oxford: Rowman and Littlefield, pp 15–30.

Sheffield, Carole. (1993) 'The invisible intruder: Women's experiences of obscene phone calls', in Pauline Bart and Eileen Geil Moran (eds) *Violence Against Women: The Bloody Footprints*, London: Sage.

Simester, A., Spencer, J.R., Sullivan, G. and Virgo, G. (2013) *Simester and Sullivan's Criminal Law: Theory and Doctrine*, Oxford: Hart.

Sisters for Change. (2017) 'Unequal regard, unequal protection', www.sistersforchange.org.uk/2017/11/20/unequal-regard-unequal-protection/

Smart, Carol. (1989) *Feminism and the Power of Law*, London: Routledge.

Smart, Carol. (2012) 'Reflection', *Feminist Legal Studies*, 20: 161–165.

Smith, Andrea. (2010) 'Beyond restorative justice: Radically organizing against violence', in James Ptacek (ed) *Restorative Justice and Violence against Women*, Oxford: Oxford University Press, pp 255–278.

Stanko, Elizabeth. (1985) *Intimate Intrusions*, London: Routledge.

Stanko, Elizabeth. (1987) 'Typical violence: Normal precaution: men, women and interpersonal violence in England, Wales, Scotland and the USA', in Jalna Hanmer and Mary Maynard (eds) *Women, Violence and Social Control*, London: Macmillan, pp 122–134.

Stanko, Elizabeth. (1990) *Everyday Violence*, London: Pandora.

Stark, Evan. (2007) *Coercive Control*, New York: Oxford University Press.

Strick, Katie. (2019) 'AirDrop has created a new weapon for cyberflashers', *Standard*, 17 September, www.standard.co.uk/comment/comment/airdrop-has-created-a-new-weapon-for-cyberflashers-a4238706.html

Strick, Katie. (2020) 'The best dating apps to use in 2020', *Standard*, 11 November, www.standard.co.uk/escapist/best-dating-apps-2020-b63270.html

Strid, Sofia, Walby, Sylvia and Armstrong, Jo. (2013) 'Intersectionality and multiple inequalities: Visibility in British policy on violence against women', *Social Politics*, 20(4): 558–581.

Suzy Lamplugh Trust. (2020) 'Cyber safety at work', 10 November, www.suzylamplugh.org/national-personal-safety-day-2020-cyber-safety-at-work

Sykes, Gresham and Matza, David. (1957) 'Techniques of neutralization: A theory of delinquency', *American Sociological Review*, 22(6): 664–670.

Taylor, Caroline and Norma, Caroline. (2011) 'The symbolic protest behind women's reporting of sexual assault', *Feminist Criminology*, 7: 24–47.

Terweil, Anna. (2020) 'What is carceral feminism?', *Political Theory*, 48(4): 421–442.

Thiara, Ravi and Gill, Aisha. (2010) *Violence against South Asian Women*, London: Jessica Kingsley.

Thiara, Ravi and Roy, Sumanta. (2020) *Reclaiming Voice*, London: Imkaan.

Thompson, Laura. (2016) '#DickPics are no joke: Cyber-flashing, misogyny and online dating', *The Conversation*, 3 February, https://theconversation.com/dickpics-are-no-joke-cyber-flashing-misogyny-and-online-dating-53843

Thompson, Laura. (2018) '"I can be your Tinder night-mare": Harassment and misogyny in the online sexual market-place', *Feminism and Psychology*, 28(1): 69–89.

Thompson, Rachel. (2019) 'It's time to stop saying "unsolicited dick pics." Here's why', *Mashable*, 19 July, https://mashable.com/article/cyberflashing-unsolicited-dick-pics-terminology/?europe=true

Tomchak, Anne. (2020) 'Megan Barton Hanson apparently makes nearly £800,000 a month selling her content on OnlyFans, but is it worth it?', *Glamour*, 16 November, www.glamourmagazine.co.uk/article/how-does-onlyfans-work

Tran, Marc. (2015) 'Combatting gender privilege and recognising a woman's right to privacy in public spaces: Arguments to criminalise catcalling and creepshots', *Hastings Women's Law Journal*, 26(2): 185–206.

Transport for London. (nd) 'Report it to stop it', www.tfl.gov.uk.

Turkle, Sherry. (2007) *Evocative Objects*, Cambridge, MA: MIT Press.

Tziallas, Evangelos. (2015) 'Gamified eroticism: Gay male "social networking" applications and self-pornography', *Sexuality and Culture*, 19(4): 759–775.

Uhrig, Noah. (2016) *Black, Asian and Minority Ethnic Disproportionality in the Criminal Justice System in England and Wales*, Ministry of Justice.

Urban Dictionary. (2020) www.urbandictionary.com.

Valentine, Gill. (1989) 'The geography of women's fear', *Area*, 21(4): 385–390.

Vera-Gray, Fiona. (2016) 'Men's stranger intrusions: Rethinking street harassment', *Women's Studies International Forum*, 58: 9–17.

Vera-Gray, Fiona. (2017a) *Men's Intrusions, Women's Embodiment: A Critical Analysis of Street Harassment*, London: Routledge.

Vera-Gray, Fiona. (2017b) 'Outlook: Girlhood, agency, and embodied space for action', in Bodil Formark, Heta Mulari and Myry Voipio (eds) *Nordic Girlhoods*, Cham: Palgrave Macmillan.

Vera-Gray, Fiona. (2018) *The Right Amount of Panic*, Bristol: Bristol University Press.

Vera-Gray, Fiona and Kelly, Liz. (2020) 'Contested gendered space: Public sexual harassment and women's safety work', *International Journal of Comparative and Applied Criminal Justice*, 44(4): 265–275.

Vera-Gray, Fiona and McGlynn, Clare. (2020) 'Regulating pornography: Developments in evidence, theory, and law', in Chris Ashford and Alexander Maine (eds) *Research Handbook on Gender, Sexuality, and Law*, Cheltenham: Edward Elgar, pp 471–483.

Vitis, Laura. (2020) 'Private, hidden and obscured: Image-based sexual abuse in Singapore', *Asian Journal of Criminology*, 15: 25–43.

Vitis, Laura and Gilmour, Fairleigh. (2017) 'Dick pics on blast: A woman's resistance to online sexual harassment using humour, art and Instagram', *Crime Media and Culture*, 13(3): 335–355.

Von Hirsch, Andrew and Jareborg, Nils. (1991) 'Gauging criminal harm: A living-standard analysis', *Oxford Journal of Legal Studies*, 11(1): 1–38.

Waling, Andrea and Pym, Tinonee. (2017) '"C'mon, no one wants a dick pic": Exploring the cultural framings of the "dick pic" in contemporary online publics', *Journal of Gender Studies*, 28(1): 70–85.

Wegerstad, Linnea. (2021) 'Theorising sexual harassment and criminalisation in the context of Sweden', *Bergen Journal of Criminal Law and Criminal Justice*.

West, Robin. (1987) 'The difference in women's hedonic lives: A phenomenological critique of feminist legal theory', *Wisconsin Women's Law Journal*, 3(81): 149–215.

Wildmoon, K.C. (2020) 'Florida man exposes himself to middle schoolers', *CrimeOnline*, 5 April, www.crimeonline.com/2020/04/05/florida-man-exposes-himself-to-middle-schoolers-during-online-math-class/

Women and Equalities Select Committee. (2018) *Sexual Harassment of Women and Girls in Public Places*, HC 701, 23 October, https://publications.parliament.uk/pa/cm201719/cmselect/cmwomeq/2148/214802.htm

YouGov. (2018) 'Four in ten female millennials have been sent and unsolicited penis photo', 16 February, https://yougov.co.uk/topics/politics/articles-reports/2018/02/16/four-ten-female-millennials-been-sent-dick-pic

Zinsstag, Estelle and Keenan, Marie. (2017) *Restorative Responses to Sexual Violence*, London: Routledge.

Index

Printed and bound by CPI Group (UK) Ltd, Croydon, CR0 4YY

25/03/2025

14647336-0002